Forty Years in the Same Pulpit

What Makes for Long Pastorates

Best wishes to
Dorothy Powell
Chris Horn

2-26-95

Forty Years in the Same Pulpit

What Makes for Long Pastorates

Chevis F. Horne

Smyth & Helwys Publishing, Inc.®
Macon, Georgia

ISBN   1-880837-89-7

Forty Years in the Same Pulpit
What Makes for Long Pastorates
by
Chevis F. Horne

Copyright © 1995
Smyth & Helwys, Publishing, Inc.®
6316 Peake Road
Macon, Georgia 31210-3960

Library of Congress Cataloging-in-Publication Data

Horne, Chevis F.
    Forty years in the same pulpit: what makes for long pastorates /
by Chevis F. Horne.
    xii + 112 pp.   6" x 9" (15 x 23 cm.)
    Includes bibliographical references.
    ISBN 1-880837-89-7
    1. Clergy—Office. 2. Church management.
    I. Title. II. Title: 40 years in the same pulpit.
    BV660.2.H63   1995   94-3567
    253—dc20   CIP

Cover design by Stephen Hefner.

Contents

To my colleagues in the ministry
among whom have been many unsung heroes

Foreword

At a time of crisis in the life of God's people, Zedekiah, king of Judah, summoned the prophet Jeremiah and asked, "Is there any word from the Lord?" Spoken, or unspoken, this is the basic question the person in the pew would address to the person in the pulpit.

Chevis Horne gathers the experience of fifty years in the ministry—forty years in a pastoral relationship with the same church—and attempts to tell pastors how year after year they can fulfill their ministry, the center of which is the faithful proclamation of God's Word.

"How do you find something to preach Sunday after Sunday, week after week?" I addressed this question to Page Kelley in the 1940s when we were both students at Southern Baptist Theological Seminary in Louisville, Kentucky. At that time Page was also the full-time pastor of a church. Having never served as a full-time pastor myself, I thought then that finding something to preach often must pose a formidable problem. This friend, who since then has served seven years as a missionary to Brazil and thirty-three years as a professor of Old Testament at Southern Seminary, answered with words of wisdom I have never forgotten: "Well, it really isn't so difficult if you stay in the Word and stay close to your people."

That statement is essentially the formula that Horne offers as he addresses the subject of what makes for long pastorates. He suggests no gimmicks and no resorting to cheap theatrics. He treats the basics with simplicity, clarity, and complete integrity.

Chevis Horne makes a good first impression and wears well. This is true whether in reference to sermons from the pulpit, lectures in a seminary classroom, or face-to-face relationships. Horne was an adjunctive professor of preaching at Southeastern Seminary for one year. He made a good first impression, he wore well, and he was invited to stay. Altogether, he taught there for about ten years. Over three years of that time, he served as seminary chaplain. I joined the seminary faculty about the time that Chevis arrived, and while we were both teaching at Southeastern, I came to know him. Horne brought excitement to the classroom and attracted large numbers of students to the chapel whenever he preached.

Chevis Horne models the kind of servant ministry that he advocates in his book. Though he frequently uses illustrations from his own experience as well as from the experience of others, he never points to himself as the model. Rather, he always points to Jesus as the one true model for ministry. Horne challenges the pastor of every church to give the church the best one has and not use it simply as a stepping stone for one's professional advancement. Always the pastor should seek to serve people, not to manipulate them or use them for one's advantage.

Keen intellectual gifts, a deep sense of God's call upon his life, a feeling of awe and wonder at the marvelous grace of God and the glory of the Gospel, a genuine love for people, a capacity for hard work, a humble recognition of his own limitations, a reliance upon the Holy Spirit, and unimpeachable personal integrity without any bombast or pretense —these are personal qualities that have enabled the author to serve one church effectively for forty years.

This is Horne's ninth book. It is a veritable treasure of systematic theology in sermon form. It may well be the author's most important work. Into this book the author pours the distilled essence of his own study and experience. Horne successfully communicates his excitement about the Gospel in all of its dimensions with no dichotomy between the so-called spiritual and secular or between the personal and corporate aspects of life.

Reading this book and seeking to embody the principles of ministry that the author so clearly enunciates should help any pastor to be a more effective minister of Jesus Christ, whether the pastor's tenure at a given church is short or long.

Robert H. Culpepper

Preface

In 1939 I stood within four months of graduating from the Southern Baptist Theological Seminary in Louisville, Kentucky. I had no idea where my place of ministry would be. If someone had pressed the question, I suppose I would have said that I would be returning to eastern North Carolina. My roots were there; my father, the late Reverend Claude Broadus Horne, was the pastor of Baptist churches in that area for many years. Eastern North Carolina had a strong appeal to me.

During that same period my friend and fellow student, Landon Maddex, was called as the pastor of the Fieldale Baptist Church in Fieldale, Virginia. He traveled to Fieldale once a month until the academic year ended. On one of his monthly visits he met J. P. McCabe, who had been the pastor of First Baptist Church in Martinsville, Virginia, for thirty years and continued as pastor there for a total of forty years.

Dr. McCabe told Landon that he was looking for an associate pastor and would appreciate his recommending a young man from the graduating class. Landon said my name came to him immediately, and he soon sent a letter of recommendation to Dr. McCabe, who then invited me to visit First Baptist Church at the end of school. I was very glad to have the opportunity and accepted the invitation.

I vividly remember the Saturday night in May that I arrived in Martinsville by bus around nine o'clock. Dr. McCabe—a short, heavy, rotund man—was standing near the bus and calling my name. We soon arrived at the parsonage that was located next to the church. There I met Mrs. McCabe, a beautiful and stately woman who was affectionately known as "Miss Sue" by the church and community. The evening was the beginning of a long and meaningful friendship with two of the finest and most unusual people I have known.

After I accepted the job as associate pastor, Mrs. McCabe invited me to live with them for a month until my permanent residence was determined. At the end of the month, however, the McCabes invited me to continue living with them, which I was happy to do. This involved taking my meals at their home as well as having a room with them. The McCabes did not have children, and I became like a son to them, and they were like a father and mother to me.

Little did I know that on the Saturday night I arrived in Martinsville I would soon begin a relationship with a church that would last for forty years—until I retired from the ministry.

I became the associate pastor of First Baptist Church, Martinsville, Virginia, in late May 1939. I left the end of October, 1942, for the chaplaincy in the armed services, but returned to the church as associate pastor in November, 1945. When Dr. McCabe retired at the end of 1947, I was elected pastor and continued in the position until I retired in June 1979. After retiring I was elected pastor emeritus.

When I went to Martinsville, I had no concept of a lengthy pastorate. I never dreamed I would stay so long. I never wanted to leave, nor did I have to. I was very happy, and across the years the church maintained vibrancy and life, although not always on the level I might have wished. I never felt that my work was done.

After I had been with the church for about twenty years I dreamed that I was called to a church in the midwest, and after much struggle I made the decision to accept. We sent our furniture ahead, and Helen and I drove there. As we crossed the corporate city limits, I suddenly realized I had made a terrible mistake. How could I have ever left First Baptist in Martinsville? I awoke in a deep depression. How relieved I was that it was only a bad dream and that I was still pastor of First Baptist Church!

I could not have stayed with most churches for such a long time, but First Baptist Church is no ordinary church. The members of First Baptist Church are unusually mature, loving, accepting, and affirming. They know they are saved by grace and that grace should be shown through graciousness in us. They fear legalism, knowing it dries up the springs of human kindness and makes people self-righteous, harsh, and judgmental. No young minister ever fell into gentler hands. I have often thought what might have happened to me in my early years in the ministry, as well as subsequent ones, if my life had not been cast among such gentle and gracious people.

In addition to the great qualities of the members, First Baptist Church has always had an open and free pulpit. Its members want their pastor to freely preach the gospel as he/she understands it, even if they do not agree. The pulpit has never been censored. I was never told what I must or must not preach.

First Baptist Church also treated my family with the highest respect. The members had the same standard for themselves as for the pastor's family. They never expected more from our children than they did from other children. They loved and affirmed us and wanted us to be free to realize our highest potential. You can understand why Helen, my two children, Chevis Jr., and Ann, and I feel affectionately about First Baptist Church.

While I have been speaking glowingly of my pastorate with First Baptist Church and am glad that I can so sincerely, I do not want to mislead you. I had my share of tension and conflict. The 1960s were turbulent. Yet, I found greater satisfaction in that period of ministry than any other. I attempted to be prophetic. It was very painful to me that the church would reject people whom Jesus had loved, for whom he had died, and whom he had accepted unconditionally. I told our people that when we rejected others, we were more the reflection of a segregated culture than we were the Church of Jesus Christ and that we could never be the Church when we kept out people whom Christ had invited. While many pastors lost their churches during that period, First Baptist Church allowed me to continue. More will be said of this later.

Now that I stand beyond the end of my ministry with First Baptist Church, I have some very clearly-defined ideas and deep convictions about long pastorates. This book is written in the strong conviction that, while the long pastorate is not without its difficulties, it has decided advantages over a short one. I will discuss both the advantages and disadvantages and give suggestions that, I believe, will enable a pastor to continue with a church for many years, avoiding a rustout and burnout, while maintaining the affection and appreciation of the congregation, and remaining fresh, vital, alive, and relevant.

I am not setting myself as a model. Yet, I hope I have learned something from a long pastorate that may be helpful to pastors who do not want to spend their lives in constant transition from one church to another. I wish to share practical advice with a strong theological undergirding.

Introduction

The Long Pastorate

Advantages of a Long Pastorate

The Alban Institute, which specializes in church growth, has published its findings on long pastorates:

> The title, *New Visions for the Long Pastorate*, originated from our discovery of powerful evidence favoring long pastorates. It is a vision that emerged despite our own initial negative assumption about long pastorates. The four researchers all changed their minds on the issue after the eight days with clergy and their spouses. In fact, we have come to see that: While all the disadvantages of a long pastorate can be managed with skill and training, few of the enormous advantages of a long pastorate are available to shorter ministries.[1]

My findings concur with the Alban conclusions; the following pages present several major advantages of a long pastorate.

Strong Relationships

The overriding advantage of a long pastorate is the opportunity to make deep, trusting, and caring relationships. Without these relationships pastors cannot accomplish much of lasting value; but it takes time to develop them.

One of the great tragedies of many churches is that the pastoral tenure is so brief. In some of our major denominations, the average is less than five years. While this is the average, many pastorates fall below the average. When many pastors are on the threshold of significant relationships with their people, they move on. As a result, pastors do not get to know the people on a deep level of trust and acceptance. In some cases, pastors can be like masked persons. Time is needed to develop trust that will allow them to remove the mask. To aid the development of deep relationships, pastors must convince the people that they are loved and cared for. Prophetic preaching, while necessary in certain situations, must be secondary.

One of the joys of being with a church for forty years is that I was able to touch the lives of several generations. When I first went to Martinsville, I performed the wedding ceremony for several couples whose parents and grandparents were still living. I saw them buy their own houses, go into business, and start their families. It was my special privilege to minister to their children, help lead them to Christ, baptize them, give them spiritual guidance, and then finally to perform their marriage ceremonies. Then the cycle began again: new house, business, children, growing into maturity, and marrying. I was privileged to minister to four generations at First Baptist Church.

Across the years I have been with those families in the most meaningful experiences of their lives. I was with them in the sharp turnings—in the way that often brought joy and fulfillment but sometimes pain, sorrow, and tragedy. I was glad with them, and I was sad with them. I laughed with them and wept with them. I was with them in the minor crises of life such as a son going into military service or a daughter going away to college. I was with them in major crises such as financial failure, divorce, serious illness, or death. In the times of crises they frequently opened doors into their lives in a way they opened to no one else. When I walked into the interior of their lives, I knew I was on holy ground.

Continuity and Stability

In a world of high mobility, where people are uprooted and on the move, where anchors have been lifted and old landmarks swept away, where relationships are fragile and easily broken, there is a deep longing for continuity, stability, and permanence. A long pastorate can help speak to this need.

The Alban Institute in its findings about long pastorates stated:

> In a period where stress and stability are the daily reality of people's lives, how fortunate many of them are to have a long-time trusted and caring friend in their parish pastor. Today, when people are so mobile, we need clergy who are models of stability. Clergy can become the anchor that keeps people grounded in reality, especially the reality of God's grace for their lives.[2]

We can learn something from Jesus' parable of the good shepherd and the hireling. Persons in long pastorates do not run when they see trouble but stay and offer the necessary security and stability in a disjointed world (see John 10:12ff).

Ministry in the Community

Long pastorates also help pastors extend their ministry beyond the limits of their churches into the life of the community. If it takes churches time to know and trust pastors, it takes communities even longer. Pastors must build trusting relationships with the community if they are to serve it in an effective way.

Every pastor should know that his or her church is not an isolated institution. It is a part of the community and draws heavily upon its life and resources. A pastor owes a debt to the community and should be eager to pay it; long tenure will enable this.

Disadvantages of a Long Pastorate

While long pastoral tenure gives the opportunity for building strong relationships, continuity and stability in the congregation, and effective ministry in the community, there are disadvantages to a long pastorate.

Pastor's Weaknesses Felt

A number of years ago I spoke with a Presbyterian minister at Princeton Theological Seminary where we were attending a conference. He had been with his church for fifteen years and was anxious for another pastorate. I asked him why he did not give the rest of his life to his church. He shocked me with his answer: "I have built my weaknesses into my church. I need to move on. Hopefully my successor will correct my weaknesses." I had never thought of it that way before but I knew immediately that he was right. Pastors with long tenure build not only personal strengths but also weaknesses into the church. They can unintentionally shape and form a church. Lazy pastors generally have lazy churches. Reserved ministers may have formal congregations. Legalistic pastors grow rigid and judgmental churches.

Potential for "Rust-out"

In long pastorates ministers can easily become complacent, grow stale, rest on the laurels and victories of other years, and dry up spiritually and intellectually. They may no longer read stimulating books, get away for conferences and continuing education, and write sermons that are fresh and stimulating. Old sermons are preached to people who have moved on from where they were when the sermon was first preached. Hackneyed, pious, and platitudinous language, no longer gripping and arresting, is unnecessarily repeated. There is no freshness, power, and expectancy in the pulpit. Such pastors continue to use pastoral capital earned and deposited in earlier years.

I have known too many pastors who have lost their zest for the pastoral task as well as spiritual vitality and vibrancy in the pulpit. They may be loved and appreciated by the congregation, but the deadness of the situation is hard to accept. The time comes when both the pastor and the congregation desire a move. If extreme action is taken, it is very painful to the congregation and may be devastating to the pastor and the pastor's family. The scenario may have been different if the pastor had been alive to the world, kept a fresh grip on the gospel, undergone intellectual discipline, and practiced a devotional life.

Danger of Burnout

Burnouts occur frequently in the lives of ministers. Some reliable studies indicate that as many as one out of five pastors are physically or emotionally burned out. Burnout may occur early in a pastor's life. I remember a theological student saying, "I sometimes feel I will be burned out before I leave this campus." Burnouts are more likely to occur during long pastorates, however.

A burnout is physical, emotional, intellectual, and spiritual exhaustion. Ministers who experience burnout feel depleted, empty, and lifeless; something has happened to the zip and zest for life. They hate to get up each morning, and depression may last throughout the day. Personal cynicism, cynicism about the church and people, and self-blame grow. Ministers experiencing burnout may doubt God's call and, though intellectually saying the gospel is good news, feel little hope. When they preach a sermon or do some good deed, they may feel that it would be just as well if the words had not been said or the service not performed. There is a terrible emptiness. Burnout in a minister's life is a real tragedy.

A long pastorate can be very draining and exhausting unless there are springs of replenishment along the way, new visions of greatness, and fresh experiences of grace.

Reasons for Short Pastorates

Many pastors cannot know the advantages and disadvantages of long pastorates since they have experienced only short tenures. What creates the restlessness in a pastor's life that causes movement from church to church, or even out of the church into some secular vocation?

An Unclear Sense of God's Call

Students may attend seminary, not essentially to prepare for the ministry but for self-discovery. Never discerning their identity or vocational abilities, they leave the seminary with a theological degree and are called to a church, but go without a real sense of God's calling. The result is deep uncertainty and a kind of tentative arrangement. Their ministry begins from a position of weakness, not strength. Ministers who do not have a clear sense of God's calling cannot experience motivation, stability, and staying power.

Disillusionment

Many pastors enter the ministry with great idealism. They have a high concept of the church. Their minds are furnished with such great images of the church as the body of Christ, a redeemed community, a reconciled fellowship, and the family of God. Their idealism gives way, however, to disillusionment and sometimes cynicism upon the discovery of realities in a church situation.

They often find pettiness, quarreling, factions, and power struggles. Frequently the church seems to be little more than the extension of its culture. Those of another race may not be accepted, and the poor and illiterate who fall below the social level of the church are not sought. The social stratification of the culture is a reality in the church. The church may seem more like a club than a redeemed fellowship having the mind of Christ. Seeking a more authentic fellowship, and failing to find it, ministers may leave the church.

Poor Self-esteem

After many years of counseling, I concluded that I had never worked with an emotionally distraught person who did not have either a poor self-image at the center of his or her problem or as a contributing factor. A professional counselor concurred with my opinion.

Many people suffer from poor self-esteem, including pastors. They often feel empty, worthless, unloved, unwanted, and restless. Pastors cannot be happy with a church when they are not happy with themselves.

Emotional Immaturity

Some pastors never grow up emotionally. A pastor may be forty years of age, yet acts like a fifteen-year-old. Such a pastor may think and behave like a child and be petulant, sensitive, and self-centered—demanding his or her way or else pouting, sulking, or withdrawing. He or she may become angry, easily explode with little provocation, and even throw temper tantrums—providing constant embarrassment to the congregation. Conflict results, and the experience will be repeated unless emotional maturity comes.

Moral Failure

Churches want to believe in the pastor. While knowing ministers are human, congregations want them to embody integrity, love, kindness, compassion, and the spirit of Jesus. Even when a church's faith in a pastor is betrayed, the members are quick to forgive and forget. They are soon ready to trust in a new pastor.

There are more moral failures in the ministry than we would like to admit. Pastors display defective character when they divulge information given to them in confidence, talk irresponsibly about members of the church to other members, engage in gossip, are careless with the truth, or are prejudiced against certain people. All too often we learn of a pastor who has been indiscrete in relating to someone in the church or community. That minister may divorce a faithful spouse in order to marry another person. When this situation occurs, the pastor usually must move on and may suffer greatly over the situation and those harmed. The tension between what the pastor should be and what he or she truly is may eventually drive the pastor from the ministry.

False Ambition

Some pastors may forget that Jesus was a servant, and that servant and minister are interchangeable terms. They may not remember that power was at the heart of Jesus' temptations and that Jesus turned from temptation to become a servant. He could have worn a crown, but he asked for a towel and basin of water. He washed and dried the dirty feet of his disciples.

Sooner or later pastors face the same kind of temptation with the same alternatives: power or servanthood. They discover how alluring and enticing power can be and how easy it is to yield. They begin to dream of the prestigious church, big salary, and ecclesiastical power—which all look decent and socially acceptable.

When they adopt the standard of success offered by the world, their role may remain a religious one, but at heart it is secular. They may speak a pious and spiritual language, but others feel the vibration of power in all that they say and do. A high, upward mobility becomes their "call." They become more interested in the church serving them than in their serving the church. In their drive for power they may use and manipulate people, even trample them beneath their feet. Such pastors cannot settle down, love, and serve the people.

Incompatibility

A church has a personality as distinct as that of the pastor. The two personalities may clash from the very beginning. The pastor may be liberal, but the church is conservative; the pastor may be innovative, and the church is traditional; the pastor may be committed to social action, while the church focus is evangelism; the pastor may be aggressive, while the church is passive. The relationship may begin in a tempest that grows in severity until the pastor is dislodged.

The time element is very important in developing compatibility. The pastor and church experience mood swings, and the mentality of both can change through the years. The pastor who had difficulty at the beginning of a ministry might have found the situation different ten years earlier or ten years later. The timing was wrong.

The personality of the pastor and the personality of the church must complement each other.

Psychological Conditioning

In many cases, both pastors and churches have been conditioned for short pastorates. Often a pastor does not expect to stay long. In other cases the church does not expect a long tenure. A lawyer, doctor, or businessperson may move into the community planning to spend his or her life there, but not the pastor.

Often the pastor is seen as little more than a transient. With this mentality, it is easy for a pastor, having had a confrontation with the deacons or other church members, to feel that the ministry there is over. Neither the pastor nor members consider working through the difficulty and developing stronger and more satisfying relationships. The church members have grown restless and demand a change, so they are willing to sacrifice the pastor to avoid the suffering of others.

Economic Factors

In most denominations, pastors are among the lowest paid professional groups. The problem may become very serious when a church imposes a certain standard of living on a pstor and his or her family. Most pastors are expected to dress acceptably and drive a decent car. If the standard of living is set beyond a pastor's income level, or if a pastor is a poor financial manager, trouble arises, particularly if a pastor borrows from parishioners and cannot pay them back. The church will not accept this practice, and sooner or later the pastor will face dismissal. Economic necessity often forces a pastor to leave the church, seeking more lucrative income from secular work.

While there are disadvantages of pastors in long tenures, findings show that strong relationships, continuity and stability, and ministry in the commuity are clearly the advantages of a long pastorate.

Notes

[1]Oswald, Habgood, Hinand, and Lloyd, *New Visions for the Long Pastorate* (Washington DC: The Alban Institute) 7.

[2]Ibid., 88.

Chapter 1

Take Hope in God's Call

Nothing can give a pastor such hope, courage, motivation, and tenacity as to know that God has called him or her to preach. The call may have come quietly, gently, or gradually; or it may have come suddenly and more dramatically. It may have been as if God laid a hand on a shoulder, shoved a person into the ways of life, and said, "Go preach my gospel." The sense of call is important to pastors, especially those who stand in the evangelical tradition. The call preserves one's ministry, despite many reasons for quitting.

A Basic Call

A theology of call clearly emerges in the Bible through the examples of numerous personalities. These men and women first experienced the basic call of all Christians. God calls us from darkness into light, from falsehood into truth, from alienation into reconciliation, from bondage into freedom, from separation into fellowship, from sin and shame into forgiveness, from lostness into salvation, from self-centered pursuits into service, and from death into life.

At a time when life is so highly individualized, we should not forget that God brought a people into existence by a call. God summoned them to be a people of special identity with a special mission. God called Abraham, not as a lone, isolated individual, but as the father of a "great nation" through whom all families of the earth would be blessed (Gen 12:1-3). God called a people, who were in fact only helpless slaves in Egypt: "When Israel was a child, I loved him, and out of Egypt I called my son" (Hos 11:1).

> But now thus says the Lord, he who created you, O Jacob, he who formed you, O Israel: "Do not fear, for I have redeemed you; I have called you by name, you are mine." (Isa 43:1)

The ones whom God called from namelessness and obscurity were to be "a priestly kingdom and a holy nation" (Exod 19:6).

In the New Testament God called another group of people: the new Israel, or the Church.

> But you are a chosen race, a royal priesthood, a holy nation, God's own people, in order that you may proclaim the mighty acts of him who called you out of darkness into his marvelous light. Once you were no people, but now you are God's people; once you had not received mercy, but now you have received mercy. (1 Pet 2:9-10)

God called them from darkness into light, found them nobodies and made out of them somebodies, and transformed their poor self-identity into "God's own people." However individual the call may be, God does not leave us in isolation, but calls us, not *from*, but *into* the life of the people of God.

The call to salvation also incorporates the call to serve and minister. The saved are to serve; they are to be ministers. Paul strongly emphasized that we are saved by grace.

> For by grace you have been saved through faith; and this is not your own doing, it is the gift of God—not because of works, lest any man should boast. (Eph 2:8-9)

In the very next verse Paul wrote: "For we are what he has made us, created in Christ Jesus for good works, which God prepared beforehand to be our way of life" (Eph 2:10). Paul further emphasized that good works are not the root of salvation as in legalism, but the fruit. Good works and service follow salvation by grace. Therefore, those whom God saves are called to be ministers. We make a tragic mistake by equating ministry with the service rendered by the ordained clergy. The *laos*, or laity, are to be ministers as well as those who have been ordained.

Imagine what would happen if on Monday morning, after the church has worshiped on Sunday, all believers moved out into every segment of the life of the community, aware that they are ministers of Christ. They would go as servants, reconcilers, and healers. They would keep open channels of communication, reach hands across all kinds of barriers, find time for those the community has forgotten, give dignity to those who are cheap in their own eyes as well as in the eyes of the world, and leave everyone they meet standing a little taller. They would go, most of them not being professional healers, knowing that they are to share Christian love, which is the greatest of all balms. One of the most important tasks of the ordained clergy is to help equip lay persons as ministers.

A Special Call

In addition to the basic call, some persons experience a special call to speak God's word. Consider the following biblical examples: Moses met God on the back side of a desert before a burning bush, the flames of which did not consume the bush. God spoke very personally to him, "Moses, Moses!" He responded "Here am I" (Exod 3:4).

Isaiah had a transforming experience as he worshiped. He beheld the great transcendent God "sitting on a throne, high and lofty" (6:1). Yet, this transcendent God was near enough to touch Isaiah's sinful lips with cleansing grace. He heard the voice of the Lord saying, "Whom shall I send, and who will go for us?" Isaiah responded, "Here am I; Send me!" (6:8).

Amos made no claim of being a professional religionist. He said he was neither a prophet nor a prophet's son. He was a lowly herdsman and a dresser of sycamore trees. He related his experience like this: "And the Lord took me from following the flock, and the Lord said to me, 'Go, prophesy to my people Israel' " (7:15).

Jeremiah remonstrated with God when God called him to be a spokesman. He pled that he was too young for such a mighty task: "Ah, Lord God! Truly, I do not know how to speak, for I am only a boy" (1:6). Then Jeremiah told how God did a very dramatic and personal thing: "Then the Lord put out his hand and touched my mouth; and the Lord said to me, 'Now I have put my words in your mouth' " (1:9).

Paul said about himself: "If I proclaim the gospel, this gives me no ground for boasting, for an obligation is laid on me, and woe to me if I do not proclaim the gospel" (1 Cor 9:16). He was compelled to preach by the living God. Paul spoke of how God had set him apart before he was born and called him by grace to speak God's word (Gal 1:15, 16).

A Call to Proclaim the Word

Pastors are called to proclaim a vital message of redemption and liberty to individuals, churches, and society as a whole. The message is a powerful one of both judgment and compassion.

An Indispensable Word

Pastors have been called to speak a word that is so indispensable, that neither those who speak it nor they who hear it can live without it. It is to life what light is to seeing, what oxygen is to breathing, what a path is to the traveler, and what truth is to the mind.

I was a regimental graves registration officer for several months during World War II. My duty was to take a contingent of soldiers and survey the area of fighting, locate the men who had been killed, and then remove their bodies to a collection point on the highway. One day one of our soldiers called to me saying, "Chaplain, here is a wounded German soldier." I saw a German soldier who, two days earlier, had suffered a serious low abdominal wound. The soldier had been dragging himself over hills beneath a hot Sicilian sun. Having no water to drink and with the loss of blood, he was literally dying from thirst. When he saw our canteens he cried out, "Vater! Vater! Vater!" Our canteens were not clean and symmetrical but soiled and battered. Yet, he knew they contained the one thing that could save his life. We are like that soldier. Men and women the world over are dying from moral and spiritual thirst, and we have the water of life!

A Word of Liberation and Freedom

In some basic sense, emancipation is the overarching theme of the Bible. Liberation and redemption are interchangeable terms. Paul took the word redemption from the world of slavery. When a slave was bought to freedom he was redeemed. It was not unusual for some humanitarian to purchase a slave to freedom.

The news of redemption is indeed a wonderful gospel. It speaks of hope to those who are in bondage—that is, all of us. We are held in bondage by forces as real as cuffs around our wrists, chains about our ankles, and prison bars that hold us. We are held by dark and sinister forces that do not love us, intend to enslave us, and eventually destroy us. While we are aware of such bonds, there is a strange perversity that causes us to remain in these destructive powers. When we are offered freedom, we choose bondage; when we are offered life, we opt for death.

The Bible is concerned with our freedom. The great events of the Bible are liberating ones. The towering event of the Old Testament is the Exodus where helpless slaves were set free by the mighty hand of God. They were set free politically, economically, socially, and spiritually. Oppressed people in our world are still looking for this kind of freedom.

The New Testament places the theme of liberation into a deeper and more comprehensive setting. People are not merely delivered from political enslavement as in the Old Testament, but are set free from the two ultimately enslaving powers: sin and death. The death and resurrection of Jesus are the two great liberating events of the New Testament. By his death Jesus liberated us from our sins; by his resurrection he set us free from our death.

The new community—the Church—made possible by the life, death, and resurrection of Jesus Christ is a liberated community. The Christian church can worship in full joy because of the work of Christ:

> To him who loves us and freed us from our sins by his blood, and made us to be a kingdom, priests serving his God and Father, to him be glory and dominion forever and ever. Amen. (Rev 1:5b, 6)

Pastors are called to continue this work of the Church and proclaim the news of liberation and joy through Christ.

A Word for the Personal and Corporate Life

The Word is extremely personal. It calls us by name and touches the deepest interior springs of our lives. Paul could say: "And the life I now live in the flesh I live by faith in the Son of God, who loved me and gave himself for me" (Gal 2:20b). Religion can never be dynamic unless it addresses the personal dimension. I am glad God loves the whole world, but I want to know God loves me. I am happy that God has named all things in creation, but I want to be sure God knows my name.

I rejoice that Jesus Christ has enough grace to cover the sins of the world, but I want the assurance that my sins are forgiven.

I shall never forget John Campbell. He was one of the finest, warmest, and most human persons I have known. I still remember the morning he made his confession of faith in Christ. A high school boy, he walked quietly down the aisle that Sunday morning, telling me he was accepting Jesus Christ as his Savior and Lord and that he wanted to be baptized into the church. Although John never told me, he related an experience he had on the morning of his confession to one of his sisters. He said that as I preached, he felt the message was for him alone, that it was as if God were calling him by name, and saying, "John, I have good news for you." John discovered how wonderfully personal the Gospel is.

The Word of God is also addressed to the corporate life—the life we live together. It is a word spoken to the family, the community, our institutions, and the culture. Our living has become so individualized that we have forgotten how corporate the Word of God is. In the Bible, it is addressed to the corporate life, the nation, and the people of God as well as the individual. The Word of God has brought into existence a great corporate reality: the church. The church is a believing, worshiping, and serving community. The individual Christian is part of the body of Christ and cannot survive alone.

A Word of Judgment and Grace

The word we preach can never be sentimentalized. It has a message of judgment—the judgment of God. This word reflects a moral structure built into the warp and woof of the universe. Its moral laws are as unrelenting and demanding as the physical laws. They have a sharp and jagged edge on which we cut and bruise ourselves. Indeed we can destroy ourselves by violating them.

God's judgment, however, does more than reflect the moral laws of the universe. It reflects God's own moral nature and tells of God's anger and wrath toward evil. Judgment is as scorching as the winds that sweep in from the desert, as exposing as a search light, and as sharp as a surgeon's knife. It cuts, bruises, and wounds.

Pastors also preach a message of grace. Where judgment hurts and injures, God's grace binds and heals. This grace can forgive the greatest sin and cleanse the foulest deed.

With this movement between judgment and grace, we have the clue to what unlocks history's meaning and charts its ways. The judgment of God marks the exit of a people from history, while God's grace calls a new people into existence—a better explanation of the movements of history than set dispensations and ages.

To those who preach: Make sure the word of judgment in your preaching comes from God's Word rather than from your own anger and hostility.

A Powerful Word

Note the images of power used to describe the Word given to Jeremiah.

> See, today I appoint you over nations and over kingdoms, to pluck up and to pull down, to destroy and to overthrow, to build and to plant. (1:10)

Paul also described the power of the Word: "For I am not ashamed of the gospel; it is the power of God for salvation to everyone who has faith, to the Jew first and also to the Greek" (Rom 1:16).

The Greek word for power is *dunamis,* from which our word dynamite comes. The gospel is the dynamite of God. While I have used the metaphor dynamite, we should remember that all power is not loud, bulky, and big. Often the greatest power is quiet and unobtrusive. The seasons shift their mighty energy without noise, the incoming tide quietly lifts the stranded barge, and the dawn breaks without the sound of a trumpet. Love is the most powerful moral force in the universe; it does not come in pomp and ceremony. Most powers, however, come with theatrics because they are not sure of themselves; they fear their weakness and seek to hide it. Love dares to come in weakness knowing that it alone is strong. Consider the example of Jesus stumbling beneath his cross on Good Friday. He looked weak and helpless, yet he was stronger than the mighty forces that marshaled their powers to put him to death.

Pastors are called to proclaim the indispensable, liberating, personal and corporate, judging and grace-full, and empowering word of God in the contemporary context. The call, indeed, is a special one.

Reflections on God's Call

God's call is a call of grace to all who will receive it. It is offered without favoritism and experienced differently by individuals. It offers great assurance, motivation, and strength in the life of ministers.

A Call of Grace

God does not call us because of natural gifts such as fine presence, good voice, attractive personality, speaking ability, or even spiritual sensitivity. Nor does God call us because we are good, deserving, and trustworthy. God calls us through grace, a mystery we can never understand.

At times we are like ancient Israel: confused about God's calling to be a special people. Moses wondered:

> It was not because you were more numerous than any other people that the Lord set his heart on you and chose you—for you were the fewest of all peoples. It was because the Lord loved you. (Deut 7:7-8)

Grace was at the center of the call. The Israelites were not selected because they were better, wiser, or more spiritual than other people. Like Moses, we may ask, "Why me, Lord?" Moses asked God, "Who am I that I should go to Pharaoh, and bring the sons of Israel out of Egypt?" (Exod 3:11). Among other things he pled that he was not eloquent; yet, God persisted.

No one has ever felt more inadequate and less worthy than Paul. He acknowledged that he was the chief of sinners. He could not forget that Christ appeared to him last of all, "as one untimely born." He confessed: "For I am the least of the apostles, unfit to be called an apostle, because I persecuted the church of God" (1 Cor 15:9). Then he pointed to the source of his call: "But by the grace of God I am what I am" (1 Cor 15:10). Mystery, yes.

God often chooses people we would not, in our pride, call. The words of Paul rebuke us: "But God chose what is foolish in the world to shame the wise; God chose what is weak in the world to shame the strong" (1 Cor 1:27). We often see how powerful weakness can become when touched by God's grace.

Response to God's Call

Some people feel they have fled God in earlier years, sometimes even rebelling against and disobeying God. When they finally accept the call to ministry, they experience peace and joy and often great emotion. A person cannot sustain such an intense emotional experience for too long, however. The glow fades, and a shadow may replace the light, causing one to wonder about the authenticity of his or her call.

When only one part of a person's life responds, the experience will be inadequate. A response of the total person is necessary. The mind should confirm it, the heart should glow over it, and the will should pledge a faithfulness to it until life's end.

If the response is only of the mind, the experience will be cold, lacking any glow or warmth. If it is only of the heart, it will be like emotional froth that will not endure. The experience of the heart should be validated by the mind and channeled by the will. If the response is only of the will, the call will be too burdensome, placing a load on the will too heavy to bear. The will needs the warmth and power of the heart. If the call is authentic, the total person must eventually respond to God in faith.

A Call Without Favoritism

Sometimes we expect God to show favoritism to those who are called. We may believe that God will continue to open doors as a sign of the call and God's continuing presence. Disappointment and disillusionment may come when those doors do not open.

During my experience of teaching and chaplaincy at a theological seminary, I talked with many students who felt great certainty and hope in their calling. A door had opened before them. But when they faced struggles with finances, illness, and marital stress, their call began to lose its glow. It further diminished when they did not secure church employment at the time of graduation. Depression, doubt, and a sense of futility for their work followed. They felt God should have treated them in a special way. Ministers should not expect such favoritism, however.

A Different Call for Each Person

We should not attempt to standardize God's call. The time, place, and manner of one's calling is different for each minister. The call may come suddenly. Like Moses, the person may know the day, place, and hour. He could have taken you to the west side of the desert of Midian near Mount Horeb to a bush and said: "God met me here. The experience was intensely personal. He called me by name." He no doubt knew the day and the hour. Isaiah could have told us: "in the year that King Uzziah died." He probably remembered the date and hour. He would have told you, "It was here that God touched my sinful lips with his grace and called me to speak his word." Amos could have done the same thing.

For other persons in the Bible, such as Peter and Paul, the call was more gradual—like the night becoming day. While Paul's conversion was sudden, his call to preach may not have been. He told us in his letter to the Galatians that after his encounter with the living Lord he did "not confer with any human being" but "went away at once into Arabia" where he may have stayed for a year or so (1:17). Maybe there he experienced a growing awareness that Christ was calling him to preach the gospel. Likewise, ministers today may sense a verification of their call through eventually knowing that happiness and fulfillment will not come from any profession other than the ministry.

A Great Source of Motivation, Assurance, and Tenacity

The assurance of God's call can prevent a rust-out or burnout. When a pastor awakes depressed on Sunday morning, not wanting to get out of bed, the sense of God's call—more than anything—will prod the person out of bed and into the pulpit. On the way to the pulpit the depression may be lifted.

Again, consider the prophet Jeremiah. He was a sensitive, brooding man, who was easily hurt. He was rejected by his generation, and put in prison, and his life was threatened. Over and over again he wanted to get away from his problems. In despair he said: "O that I had in the desert a traveler's lodging place, that I might leave my people and go away from them!" (9:2). Eventually he had one of those dreaded burnouts and did not want to preach anymore. Listen to his soliloquy:

> If I say, "I will not mention him, or speak any more in his name," then within me there is something like a burning fire shut up in my bones; I am weary with holding it in, and I cannot. (20:9)

Jeremiah could not forget the day that God put the Word on his lips and told him to speak it. In this call, he found the resilience to continue his ministry.

God's call will prevent burnout and lead ministers through the dark night into a brighter and more hopeful day. It will provide strong motivation and a high purpose throughout the years of ministry. Pastors can take hope in God's call. It is a call of grace, a gift. When responding to this gift of God—a gift that is different for each person—pastors should not expect favoritism, but rather, assurance from God for the journey.

Chapter 2

Be a Person for Others

Dietrich Bonhoeffer, Hitler's famous prisoner, dubbed Jesus as the "man for others." Jesus was indeed a man for others, a servant. He never won a victory he could not share. He violated social propriety and ran rough-shod over venerable traditions in order to meet the needs of people. The sick man who needed healing was more important than Sabbath ritual. The dinner table was the last social barrier that he broke down—he ate with publicans and sinners. He died that people might have forgiveness of sins and was resurrected that we might live. He is now at the right hand of God making intercession for us. To emulate Christ, a pastor must be a person for others and follow the model of Jesus by loving, caring, and serving others.

Clyde Fant and William Pinson in their impressive work, *20 Centuries of Great Preaching,* concluded that one thing binds together great preachers more than anything else: They care for people. They wrote,

> The sermons in this study demonstrate the relevance with which these men preached to the specific needs of people and to the issues of their day. Not a one of them was lost in abstract theology, aimless piety, or ranting exhortation. There is no artificial division in their preaching between "ethics" and "evangelism." The essential fact is they cared. They cared about people, their pain and grief—whether spiritual, physical, moral, or social—and they addressed themselves to that.[1]

To model one's ministry after Jesus, a pastor must love people, discover their worth, believe in them, serve them, be present with them, identify with them, and develop a pastoral church.

Love People

Not long before he left them, Jesus told his disciples, "I give you a new commandment, that you love one another. Just as I have loved you, you also should love one another" (John 13:34).

What was new about the commandment? Even people who had never heard of Jesus knew they should love people rather than hate them—just as they knew they should tell the truth rather than lie, protect property rather than destroy it, and save life rather than kill.

The second part of the commandment was very new, however. The world saw in Jesus a radically new love. He loved not only the beautiful, healthy, lovable, and good people; he also loved the broken, marred, sick, and sinful persons. The objects of his love could not merit his love, nor did they have to. His love flowed like an artesian well, a love freely bestowed and given unconditionally. It asked for nothing in return and made no demands upon its recipients. This love would go any distance to find the lost, descend any depth to lift up the fallen, and bear any pain to heal the broken. The New Testament calls it agape—the love that gives all.

One of the loveliest scenes in the New Testament is recorded in John 21 when the resurrected Lord appeared along the Sea of Galilee at the breaking of the morning. He saw seven of his disciples who had spent a futile night fishing. They were weary and discouraged. After Jesus hosted a breakfast, he and Simon Peter strolled along the seashore that was haunted by many pleasant memories. Jesus asked Simon Peter, "Simon, son of John, do you love me more than these?" He asked him not once, but twice, even three times. Each time Peter gave a positive response, and Jesus said to him: "Feed my lambs," "Feed my sheep," and "Feed my sheep." Underlying that experience is a basic question that never surfaces: "Simon Peter, will you be a good pastor?" Yet, Jesus never asked, "Will you love people?" but "Will you love me?" If Peter loved Jesus best of all, then he would love people the way Jesus did. Here is the unique dimension of being a pastor—seeing beauty and worth not seen before and loving in a unique way.

The images used in the conversation with Simon Peter are pastoral. Pastor is a term that means shepherd. In Isaiah we find a picture of God as shepherd: "He will feed his flock like a shepherd; he will gather the lambs in his arms, and carry them in his bosom, and gently lead the mother sheep" (40:11).

Jesus said, "I am the good shepherd. The good shepherd lays down his life for the sheep" (John 10:11). The early church people saw their pastors as shepherds. "Tend the flock of God that is your charge" (1 Pet 5:2), wrote Peter. Was Peter remembering the conversation he had with

Jesus many years earlier along the Sea of Galilee? It was there he had promised to tend his sheep.

The term pastor is tender—denoting compassion, caring, healing, and nurturing. Seward Hiltner wrote:

> As we understand it, shepherding from the biblical period to our day is unique to Christianity. Other high religions have spiritual directors of one kind or another who deal with people as individuals or in small groups. But dealing with people in terms of shepherding, the essence of which looks toward healing in a holistic sense, is unique to Christianity and Judaism, and even in Judaism developments since biblical days have been quite different from that in Christianity.[2]

In tending the sheep, the shepherd/pastor must be steadfast. The story is told of when barbarians were overrunning North Africa and making ready to besiege Hippo where Augustine was pastor and bishop. People were fleeing the city, but Augustine said: "It is not right for the shepherd to flee when the flock is left; the priest of God must stay at his post."[3] Today the universal voices of Christian ministers affirm Augustine's conviction.

Love and caring are truly at the heart of a pastor's ministry. Bishop James Armstrong wrote that P. M. Boyd was "the greatest, most sensitive shepherd of souls I have ever known." As Boyd's associate for three years, Armstrong said: "I saw him work with people, suffer and bleed with people, love people." Boyd told Armstrong what to say at his funeral: "Tell them I love God, the Methodist Church, and people— especially children."[4]

When I think of a pastor's love, I remember the words of a visiting preacher many years ago: "I observe how the children speak to their pastor along the corridors of the church. That tells me a lot about a pastor and how he cares for his people."

A former student told me of visiting a church as a prospective pastor. When I asked him how things went, he seemed disappointed and believed the pulpit search committee was ill-prepared and did not know the right questions to ask. But he said, "They seemed to say that if I would love them they would love me." He was subsequently called to the church, and his experience with them gave evidence of the importance of a pastor loving the people.

Discover the Worth of People

A good pastor will love people and believe in their inestimable value—signposts of true Christianity. William Barclay said that Christianity is the most uplifting thing, not only in the whole world, but in the entire universe:

> It was the glory of Christianity, that it made people who were things into real men and women, nay more, into sons and daughters of God; it gave those who had no respect their self-respect; it gave those who had no life, life eternal; it told men that even if they did not matter to men they still mattered intensely to God. It told men who, in the eyes of the world, were worthless, that, in the eyes of God, they were worth the death of God's only Son.[5]

Peter talked about how the members of the early church, many of whom had been nobodies, became somebodies. He observed, "Once you were no people, but now you are God's people; once you had not received mercy, but now you have received mercy" (1 Pet 2:10).

Paul spoke eloquently of how the low and inferior, those who were exploited and discriminated against, had been lifted up and given a new status and dignity in the church. He wrote, "There is no longer Jew nor Greek, there is no longer slave nor free, there is no longer male nor female; for all of you are one in Christ Jesus" (Gal 3:28). Women stood with their husbands. Slaves were given recognition and responsibility in the church. Their gifts were recognized and developed as nowhere else.

According to the brief letter of Philemon, Paul was sending Onesimus, a runaway slave whom he had won to Christ in Rome, back to his master Philemon. Paul did not cry out against slavery, but announced a principle that would some day break the yoke of slavery. Paul urged Philemon to accept Onesimus back "no longer as a slave but more than a slave, a beloved brother" (v. 16).

Near the end of the first century, a man by the name of Onesimus was bishop of the church at Ephesus, the most prestigious church in Asia Minor. Some scholars believe he was Onesimus, the runaway slave, while others dispute it. Whether or not the story is true, slaves were given a new dignity in the light of Christian faith and a new value in the fellowship of the Christian church.

Paul spoke of the church as being the body of Christ, with all members making a worthwhile contribution. One of his most striking and significant statements was: "On the contrary, the members of the body that seem to be weaker are indispensable" (1 Cor 12:22).

Pastors should consider the value of each congregant. People are not to be used as tools or manipulated as means to an end. Pastors should not focus on programs but rather its people. They should not use people to build up the church, but rather use the church to build up people. On Sunday morning pastors may preach to people who, despite their worth, do not see themselves as worthy. Pastors have the privilege to accept and affirm people in such a way that they eventually see themselves as successful.

Believe in People

Because of the actual or potential worth of people and their possibilities when they are touched by God's grace, pastors should believe in people even when they do not believe in themselves. Ministers should see beauty in individuals when they cannot see it in themselves, and display faith in them to help draw out their potential and convince them of their worth.

Remember that Jesus called ordinary, unlikely people to be his disciples. He did not go to the theological seminary at Jerusalem, seek out the dean, and say, "I should like for you to give me the names of the twelve brightest young men in this year's graduating class." Rather, Jesus went to the seashore and called rough, unlettered fishermen. He even went by a tax office and called Matthew, who bore the terrible social stigma of being a tax collector. Jesus looked beneath the rough exteriors and saw that they were open and teachable. He saw possibilities in them that no one else had discovered.

I once had a college professor who saw possibilities in me I could never see in myself. When I doubted myself, he kept on believing in me, and never gave up on me. Whatever I may do or become I will owe more to him than I can ever express. Likewise, pastors should see the best in people and support them during self-doubt.

Serve People

Years ago I visited the famous Hall of Mirrors at Versaille, France. It is a long hall lined on either side and at both ends with tall mirrors. I walked the full length several times. I saw my image reflected in the mirrors, and as I looked down the hall I saw mirrors picking up my image from others. That experience represents a parable of life. We are all tempted to live a mirrored life, to see our faces in situations and other people. We can easily exploit situations and use people to our advantage. Pastors do not escape this temptation.

It is a great hour of grace when the mirrors are turned into windows through which I look out upon our world and see faces like my face, marked with hope and despair, laughter and pain. What an experience of grace when I realize as a pastor that my main business in life is to love and serve those people!

When I was in college I was initiated into a fraternity. The fraternity brothers blindfolded me and asked me to remove my shoes and socks. No one talked; there was an eerie quietness. I experienced more than suspense, however; I was frightened. Then, a member came by and washed my feet; another one dried them. The experience was almost overpowering. Even though that event was fifty years ago, the memory returns intermittently with almost the same freshness and power as when I experienced it. If a ritual of service can have such power, what about the deed of service? Pastors have such a privilege to serve people.

Pastors can learn from the great educator and scientist, George Washington Carver. The epitaph on his tombstone in Tuskegee, Alabama, reads:

> George Washington Carver—died in Tuskegee, Alabama, January 5, 1943. A life that stood out as a gospel of Self-Forgetful Service. He could have added fortune to fame, but caring for neither, he found happiness and honor in being helpful to the world.

Whatever pastors do, even administration, should be done in loving service to people that will affirm them and help them grow.

Serving people may involve risks and taking chances, however. Jesus took risks for the sake of people. He talked with the Samaritan woman, a person of bad reputation, while his disciples went to a nearby town for food. His disciples were shocked when they returned: "They were astonished that he was speaking with a woman" (John 4:27). A man dared not talk to a woman in public. A common word of advice from rabbis was: "Let no one talk with a woman in the street, no, not with his own wife." The disciples were concerned about this indiscretion because it could cause gossip and bring shame on Jesus. Fortunately, he was willing to take the risk for the sake of the woman.

Today pastors may experience a similar risk if they visit parishioners unaccompanied. While pastors should not be indiscrete, at times they must be concerned enough about the pain of people to see the wrong person, at the wrong place, and at the wrong time. Service involves risk.

Be with People

A few years ago we were talking about a theology of presence. God is present in all of the world and universe. Likewise, we are called to be with people who need us, regardless of what we may or may not say or do. People who have experienced a serious crisis may forget what their pastor said, but they will never forget his or her presence.

Pastors should strike cadence with people, walk with them, call them by name, and reach out and touch them. Ministers are called to be with them in the sharp turnings of life that bring surprise, sometimes joy, and sometimes pain. They are to be present when life matters most, during the joyful times—marriage, the birth of a baby, and success—as well as in pain and tragedy—divorce, financial loss, when a child proves disappointing, sickness, and death.

Sensitive pastors are especially aware that in a serious crisis, people open doors they have never opened before. When pastors enter a door in times of crisis, the way may lead to the most interior dimensions of a person's life. Pastors should never betray a person's trust or confidence. To do so would disqualify them as good pastors.

When Jesus was ready to leave his disciples, he found them sad, lonely, and depressed. He told them he would send them the Paraclete—the comforter, counselor, strengthener, helper, advocate, champion—one to work beside them. Pastors are called to be a kind of Paraclete, in other words, one who stands beside their congregation. Caring pastors stand beside the weak to strengthen them, the faltering to steady them, the fallen to lift them up, the uncertain to assure them, the grieving to comfort them, the lonely to be their friend, the wayward to guide them, and the hopeful to help clarify their vision.

Identify with People

Few things, if any, have a clearer theological basis than that of identification. In the Incarnation, God took our frail and fragile form and became one with us. Jesus achieved identification with others as no one else has. He knew what it was to take into his own life the pain and joy, laughter and sorrow, and shame and sin of others.

Mother Teresa has given a prayer in which she sees Jesus identified with those who suffer:

> Dearest Lord, may we see you this day in the persons of your sick, and whilst nursing them, minister to you. Though you hide behind the unattractive disguise of the irritable, the exacting, the unreasonable, may I still recognize you and say: "Jesus, my patient, how sweet it is to serve you." Lord, give me your seeing faith, then my work will never be monotonous. I will ever find joy in honoring the fancies and gratifying the wishes of all poor sufferers.[6]

In his parable of the Last Judgment, Jesus pictured the hungry, thirsty, naked, homeless, sick, and prisoners who will be the witnesses on that last great day. Yet, he did not say that *they* were unfortunate, but that *he* was.

> For I was hungry and you gave me food, I was thirsty and you gave me something to drink, I was a stranger and you welcomed me, I was naked and you gave me clothing, I was sick and you took care of me, I was in prison and you visited me. (Matt. 25:35-36)

He was so identified with all types of people that their hunger, thirst, nakedness, homelessness, sickness, and shame of prison became his own.

When he met the living Lord along the Damascus road, Paul heard Jesus ask, "Saul, Saul, why do you persecute me?" (Acts 9:4). Paul could have easily remonstrated with Jesus: "Lord, why do you say I persecuted

you? I have never even seen you. I grew up in Tarsus and you in Nazareth, and they are far apart. I did not accuse you, nor did I drive spikes
into your hands." He would have heard Jesus reply: "But you persecuted
my followers, and I am identified with them. When you whipped them,
you beat me. The lashes that fell on their backs cut me. When you put
them in jail, you put me behind prison bars."

St. Francis of Assisi, whose gentle and loving life still blesses our
world, came from a wealthy family. One day when he was riding outside
the city he saw a leper who was a mass of running sores, a horrible and
repulsive sight. Ordinarily the fastidious Francis would have turned from
this wretched piece of humanity but, moved by a strange impulse he did
not understand, he dismounted from his horse and took the leper into his
arms. When he did, behold, the face of the leper became the face of
Christ. In embracing the leper, he took Christ into his arms.

Henri J. W. Nouwen, with penetrating insight into what makes a
pastor authentic, wrote:

> Whether he tries to enter into a dislocated world, relate to a convulsive
> generation, or speak to a dying man, his service will not be perceived
> as authentic unless it comes from a heart wounded by the suffering
> about which he speaks.
>
> If there is any posture that disturbs a suffering man or woman, it
> is aloofness. The tragedy of the Christian ministry is that many who are
> in great need, many who seek an attentive ear, a word of support, a
> forgiving embrace, a firm hand, a tender smile, or even a stuttering con-
> fession of inability to do more, often find their ministers distant men
> who do not want to burn their fingers . . . . Who can save a child from
> a burning house without taking the risk of being hurt by the flames?
> Who can listen to a story of loneliness and despair without taking the
> risk of experiencing similar pains in his own heart and even losing his
> precious peace of mind? In short: who can take away suffering without
> entering it?[7]

Nouwen is correct. Only those who have had the courage to enter suffering can take it away. Only those who get beneath burdens can lift
them. Only those who have been wounded can heal. The deepest level of
ministry can only be achieved as pastors identify with the people. They
must stand in their shoes, look at the world through their eyes, laugh and
weep with them, and feel despair and hope with them. As congregants

hurt, pastors also suffer; as persons are wounded, ministers know the sharp barbs of life, too.

Develop a Pastoral Church

A pastoral church is one that is led by persons who have a caring heart for others and have acquired pastoral skills. Pastoral ministers feel that Christ has called them, and that they are to be his hands and feet, his love and affirmation, and his acceptance and healing in our world. They are not limited to the church walls nor locked within sacred hours. They are free and open for service in the world. Because they are mobile, they can make a quick response to SOS calls wherever they hear them. Yet, they know the value of church worship, teaching, and fellowship. The members hear the Word of God in fresh and contemporary terms, experience the cleansing and renewal of worship, catch a new vision of their world as seen in the light of God, have old skills of ministry refurbished, and acquire new ones. They feel the strength of hands that reach out, voices that call, and feet that strike cadence with them.

Developing a pastoral church requires maturity and selflessness. Immature and insecure pastors may use and manipulate people. They tend to be possessive and enjoy having people come to them for counseling and other forms of ministry. They may be slow to give up a counselee, and in subtle ways they keep the person coming back, thinking they are meeting the needs of others, when in fact, they are meeting their own needs. Similarly, such pastors insist on being in the limelight and on center stage.

John the Baptist could have acted in such an immature and self-centered manner. During his best days hundreds of people came to listen to him, but times changed, and the crowds no longer came. I can imagine him, a lonely, solitary figure, along the banks of the Jordan. Then one day a disciple announced to him: "Rabbi, the one who was with you across the Jordan, to whom you testified, here he is baptizing, and all are going to him" (John 3:26). That observation could have so easily aroused jealousy, but it did not. Because John was mature and not easily threatened, he responded, "He must increase, but I must decrease" (3:30).

Pastors who wish to grow a pastoral church, a church for others, must be willing to decrease that the church may increase. They will rejoice in the fact that the church has not only one minister but 400.

Nouwen has observed that when nothing or nobody is waiting for you, there is little chance to survive the struggles of life. Thousands of people commit suicide because no one is waiting for them. According to Nouwen,

> There is no reason to live if there is nobody to live for. A man can keep his sanity and stay alive as long as there is at least one person who is waiting for him.[8]

In growing a pastoral church, pastors may be sure that the church creates a future for many persons who believe they have none. Such a church will be waiting for them as the years unfold.

There is excitement and a sense of reward in being a pastor for others, a shepherd for Christ's sheep. The joy intensifies when the church is pastoral—a church for others.

Notes

[1]Clyde Fant and William Pinson, *20 Centuries of Great Preaching*, 13 vols. (Waco: Word Books, 1971)13: vii.

[2]Seward Hiltner, *The Christian Shepherd* (Nashville: Convention Press, 1973) 14-15.

[3]Augustine, Source Unknown.

[4]James Armstrong, *Telling the Truth: The Foolishness of Preaching in a Real World* (Waco: Word Books, 1977) 67.

[5]William Barclay, *The Letters to the Corinthians* (Philadelphia: Westminster, 1954) 24.

[6]Mother Teresa, Source Unknown.

[7]Henri J. M. Nouwen, *The Wounded Healer* (Garden City NY: Doubleday & Co., Inc., 1972) xiv, 71-73.

[8]Ibid., 66.

Chapter 3

Know the Importance of the Pastorate

Many people today say that the stature of the pastor has diminished, the image of the vocation is blurred and poorly defined, and the prophetic voice is less effective. Despite these claims, the pastor is indispensable— just as the "parson" in early American life was the most respected and influential person in the community.

I was reminded of the importance of a pastor's work in 1980 at the close of my interim pastorate. The pulpit search committee wanted a person who would lead the congregants, counsel them in difficult times, be with them in sickness, comfort them in sorrow, marry their young, say the last rites over their beloved dead, quicken the conscience of the community, preach the good news of the gospel, and be a symbol of what the church has been throughout centuries. These high expectations of a pastor have been confirmed in many ways.

I attended a homecoming at one of our local churches a few years ago. A deacon, who is a very thoughtful and highly respected man in the community, said just before the worship service, "The people who have made our area strong and progressive have been our pastors more than anyone else."

I once heard George A. Buttrick, who is without dispute one of the really great preachers, say, "If I had a hundred lives to live I would want to give all of them to the ministry."

I also heard George W. Truett, with his powerful pulpit presence, say, "If I had a thousand lives to live I would want to be a preacher of Jesus Christ in all of them."

Recently my church in Martinsville celebrated my fiftieth anniversary in the life of the church and community. In reflection, I can truthfully say with Buttrick and Truett that I would like to do it all over again.

I affirm the importance of the pastoral role because it represents the oldest vocation, is associated with one of the most enduring and important institutions, gives precedence to the proclamation of God's Word, and offers numerous opportunities for healing and ministry in times of change and crises. Pastors indeed have a unique calling.

The Oldest Vocation

Wayne E. Oates wrote: "The Christian pastor enters the responsibilities of his crisis ministry in the strength of the oldest calling among men."[1] No single government, family, or economic system has survived as long as the church. These institutions are born, continue for a while, grow old, die, and then new ones start. Despite the reforms, radical changes, and new directions, the church has maintained its self-identity. It is constant and, in its most radical hours, has been able to confess that Jesus Christ is Lord. Similarly, modern pastors join hands with those of the past in great strength and unbroken continuity.

An Important Institution

Although the church can be false and hypocritical, and often falls short of its own hopes and Christ's expectations for it, it has been indispensable for our world. Imagine moving to a community that has great educational, cultural, and economic advantages and finding it has no churches. Educational, cultural, and economic values alone cannot integrate one's life into wholeness and health like spiritual values can.

The church addresses the deepest and most fundamental level of human life. It keeps the wonder and mystery of life alive. In a world where the ceilings of life become oppressively low, the church points to height, wonder, and mystery.

In a world of flux, change, and decay, the church speaks of eternal and everlasting verities. It makes a radical claim: God has spoken and given the Word to the church to proclaim the good news to the world. The church announces where grace can be found, where forgiveness is offered, and where separation and estrangement can be reconciled. It is a fellowship where there is love, acceptance, affirmation, and emphasis on the worth of individuals. In its most authentic form, it overcomes the barriers that men and women in their pride and arrogance, have constructed. The church draws people from all races, classes, nationalities, and cultures to a oneness in Christ. It continues to be the most important institution for its life-giving mission of meeting the deepest and most fundamental needs in our world today.

Proclaiming the Word

Pastors are called to be heralds of glad tidings and announcers of good news. They are proclaimers of a gospel of grace and hope, the best news our world has ever heard or will ever hear.

The importance of proclaiming God's Word is demonstrated in the life of Jeremiah who was called by God early in life. When he remonstrated with God that he was but a child and was not up to the task, God did a very dramatic and convincing thing: God touched Jeremiah's lips, telling him that he had put the word in his mouth. Though at times Jeremiah wanted to give up his calling of proclamation, the Word of God burned in his heart and would not be quenched. He continued preaching.

Washington Gladden also knew the significance of speaking the word:

> I have never tried to do anything else but preach. I have had no other ambition. If I can preach the highest truth I know clearly and convincingly, that, I know, will be the best service I can render to my kind.[2]

The man or woman who truly knows the importance of the pastorate, knows that at the heart of God's call is an unrelenting urgency to proclaim the good news of God.

Opening Doors to Healing

Wayne Oates wrote of the function of the pastor:

> The role and function of a minister have, throughout the centuries of Christian culture, bred into the deeper levels of consciousness of those whom he serves. Therefore, he has symbolic power as well as personal influence, and the symbolic power of his role gives him strength far beyond his own personal appeal to people. Paul described it well when he said: "We are ambassadors for Christ, God making his appeal through us" (2 Cor 5:20). The pastor represents and symbolizes far more than himself, he represents God the Father; he is the emissary of a specific church.[3]

Indeed, pastors have unique opportunities to open doors to healing due to the perceptions of their role. When pastors visit a sick person in the hospital, they represent the church with its long years of faith, worship, and ministry. They also represent a long tradition of hope and healing, lifting the spirit of the patient.

The role of the pastor as healer is also apparent in times of grief. The deceased person and pastor may not have known each other, but the family will turn to the pastor for comfort and to conduct the funeral. The door to ministry is open because of the appreciation and respect for the pastoral role and the level of affirmation and trust the pastor has established. Thus, pastors can unlock the doors to the most intimate, personal, and interior areas of life. The pastoral function and offering of personal worth as a friend are powerful keys.

Meeting People in Times of Change and Crises

Great religion meets people in times of change, great decisions, pain, loss, and other crisis situations. Such religion says to people: "I will meet you at the turning points of life. I will stand with you at the confusing intersections of life. I will be with you when life matters most."

The examples for ministry during life changes and problems are found in the Bible. The parents and friends of Jesus ministered to him in their own way at various stages of his life. Jesus demonstrated actual physical and spiritual healing, grief ministry, and counsel to those who were hurting and facing problems. The disciples and members of the early church continued this function of meeting needs as they arose.

Pastors are representatives of Christ and the Church. They are called to minister to people in crises—to stand with them through the sudden jolts and radical turnings in life, to empathize in the great acquisitions and losses of life, to feel their hope and despair, and to laugh or weep with them. Through crisis ministry, pastors have the opportunity to develop special relationships.

The Uniqueness of the Pastorate

Reinhold Niebuhr, the great Protestant theologian, began his ministry as a pastor in Detroit, Michigan. He was an extremely shy and sensitive man, and in his early years found visitation very difficult. Yet, as he became deeply involved in the lives of his people, he found it almost impossible to break away from them. When at last he decided to leave the pastorate for teaching, he said, "There is nothing quite like the pastoral relationship."[4] Truly, the pastoral relationship is quite unique. It can be a loving, accepting, affirming, and serving one.

I knew how wonderful that relationship could be when I attended a surprise birthday party for John Powers, a black pastor in our city. The event was a carefully guarded secret until John entered the sanctuary, where a host of church members and friends were gathered to wish him a happy birthday. The master of ceremonies at the dinner was a fine young businessman. Among other things, he said: "My father died when I was a little boy, and Reverend Powers has been like a father to me. I couldn't have made it without him."

The importance and significance of the pastoral role cannot be overstressed. If pastors take seriously their calling and the church they represent, proclaim God's Word with fervor, and minister to people in times of need and at their level, they can truly be God's agents for changing lives.

Notes

[1]Wayne E. Oates, *The Christian Pastor* (Philadelphia: Westminster Press, 1951) 43.

[2]Clyde E. Fant, Jr., and William M. Pinson, Jr., *20 Centuries of Great Preaching*, 13 vols. (Waco: Word Books, 1971) 6:181.

[3]Oates, 43.

[4]Reinhold Niebuhr, *Leaves from the Notebook of a Tamed Cynic* (Chicago: Willett, Clark, and Calby, 1929) 3.

Chapter 4

Do Well the Most Holy Task

As leaders of worship, pastors will never have a higher privilege, a more awesome challenge, nor a holier task. Worship leadership requires keen skills and a great sensitivity, both to God and people. But with the human frailties of awkwardness and clumsiness, how can pastors handle sacred things, speak of unseen and eternal realities, and lead people into the presence of a holy and loving God?

Pastors are called to be more than clever leaders of worship, displaying finesse and polish and attempting to manipulate God. Our best techniques and methods of worship leadership are to no avail unless they open persons to God and help tap springs of spiritual life. They should be enablers that unclutter the lives of individuals, clarify their vision, and make them available to God.

Pastors must not be so busy leading worship that they personally fail to worship and enter into the presence of God. Like members of their congregations, they can learn the nature and purpose of worship, its basic movements, and esssential experiences. In worship pastors can receive a vision of the evangelistic task, hear the prophetic voice, and feel the nurturing power of their pastoral duties.

The Nature and Purpose of Worship

Worship is primarily an experience involving God. It is essentially spiritual. Though we may enter our sanctuaries or private places of prayer for introspection, contemplation of moral values, or heightening our social awareness, they are not the foci of worship. We worship to offer prayer, adoration, praise, thanksgiving, and confession to God.

Henry Sloane Coffin wrote:

> The primary element in Christian worship is this adoring recognition of the most dear Father, the August Lord of all worlds. Every service should begin by setting men before him.[1]

Similarly, William Barclay said that the first test of worship is whether or not it makes us feel the presence of God.

The term "worship" is of ancient Anglo-Saxon origin: *woerthscipb*, which means to ascribe worth. God is a God of worth and is more than worthy of our best worship. God is beauty without marring, goodness without evil, truth without error, power without ruthlessness, justice without prejudice, mercy without sentimentality, light without darkness, love without bitterness, and life without mortality.

Pastors should remember that most persons have an insatiable hunger for God. In our best moments we know what the psalmist meant: "As a deer longs for flowing streams, so my soul longs for you, O God. My soul thirsts for God, for the living God" (Ps 42:1-2).

During the French Enlightenment, a sophisticated cynic said to a simple peasant who was working in his fields, "It is just a matter of time before religion will be dead. We shall soon pull down your steeples and tear down your churches." "But," replied the peasant, "you cannot pull down the stars."

We are incurably religious, and at the heart of our religious nature is the impulse to worship and serve God. Of course, at times we may misread the signals of our hearts and worship false gods; yet, we are dimly aware that we were made by God and for God. Pastors should be strengthened by the realization that during the hour of worship they will appeal to something deep and primordial in the human spirit.

In addition to the primary purpose of worship that involves the focus on God, the secondary purpose is of social awareness—how we see our brothers and sisters, and how faithful we are during the week to the vision of our world we received in the sanctuary. We face a strange paradox in Christian worship. While worship is basically spiritual, the test of its validity is social in nature. The test of what happens on Sunday morning is the way we live in our world during the week. The test of the altar is the workbench. As we leave our sanctuaries, God calls us to administer justice, love, and mercy in the world. Our worship is never validated until we apply it.

The prophet Amos lived during a time when religion was popular but void of ethical and social dimensions. The sanctuaries were crowded, the liturgy was moving, and the voice of the preacher was soothing and comforting. People who had cheated in the market place brought their ill-gotten gain and dropped it generously into the treasury of the Lord. Religion, rather than convicting their conscience, was like an opiate that dulled their moral sensibilities. They were unfaithful in marriage, the powerful exploited the weak and poor, the businessmen lied and cheated in the market place, justice failed in the courts, and the formalism of the sanctuary laid a cold and deadening hand on the spirits of the people. Amos heard God say that he would reject their worship, no matter how impressive:

> Take away from me the noise of your songs; I will not listen to the melody of your harps. But let justice roll down like waters, and right-eousness like an ever-flowing stream. (5:23-24)

Jesus told us that the final judgment of God would be concerned with justice and mercy, not superficial and formal religion. In Matthew 25 where the Last Judgment is depicted, the great questions will not be: Were you orthodox? Did you believe the scriptures? Were you faithful in worship? Rather, we will be asked: Did you feed the hungry, clothe the naked, give water to the thirsty, take in the homeless, visit the sick, and comfort those in prison? Like our biblical counterparts, only by prac-ticing justice and living righteous lives beyond the sanctuary will our worship in the sanctuary be acceptable.

Basic Movements of Worship

While worship should be spontaneous, it is not to be haphazard. Worship has its own rhythm, pattern, and movements that are discernible and de-finable. Many theologians believe our finest model for the public worship of God is found in Isaiah 6, where Isaiah's transforming experience in the Temple is described. There were four basic movements in that experi-ence. By setting these movements in an order of worship, the congrega-tion can interpret the progression of worship.

A Vision of God

Above the change, flux, and instability of his world Isaiah "saw the Lord sitting upon a throne, high and lofty" (v. 1). Above God were seraphims who sang antiphonally, "Holy, holy, holy is the Lord of hosts; the whole earth is full of his glory" (v. 3).

No authentic worship occurs without a vision of God, yet we cannot produce this vision of God through our own effort. God takes the initiative and enables us to experience God's presence. God touches our blind eyes that we may behold God's beauty and majesty. Worship is a response to God's overtures. The psalmist knew this: " 'Come,' my heart says, 'Seek his face!' Your face Lord, do I seek. Do not hide your face from me" (27:8-9a).

The People's Offering to God

Isaiah, probably a young courtier or priest, worshiped God in the Temple during a time of crisis. King Uzziah, a good king, had died; political chaos was in the land; and the future of the nation was uncertain. There was likely inward turmoil in Isaiah's life that reflected the outward chaos. He felt anxious and troubled as he entered the temple of worship.

Isaiah did not go empty-handed; he brought gifts. Whether he was a courtier or priest had some bearing on what he offered. He definitely brought a memory of a religious past and a story of God's redemptive deeds. He probably offered some more tangible gifts. In any case, he brought his life—weak, frightened, uncertain, and distraught. He obviously took a wistfulness to that hour. He was open to a new direction, a new life, and a new vocation. We, too, make offerings and gifts to God in our worship. We sing hymns of praise, adoration, and consecration; and express prayers of adoration, thanksgiving, confession, intercession, and petition.

In speaking of prayer as an offering to God, mention should be made of how important the pastoral prayer can be in worship. Pastors can portray the role of priests moreso when they offer the pastoral prayer than at any other time. Through it they can truly represent the people to God. The prayer should reflect deep insight into the lives of the people as well as great concern and feeling for them. Pastors should give the prayer not from the attitude of aloofness from the congregation, but from that of walking with them. With clarity and compassion, confession is made to God for the weaknesses and hopes of the congregation as well as for oneself as minister. The pastoral prayer should express such depth that people in the congregation will say to themselves: "How does the pastor know me so well? The prayer spoke of my condition better than I could and expressed what I have longed to say but have never known how."

We also bring gifts from our common life and toil to which we have given the best energy and hours of the week. We bring these gifts, knowing that God is not a despiser of common things. Jesus was a carpenter whose hands were calloused by the use of the hammer and saw. These gifts remind us that we do our common work in God's world where we are stewards through years that are too brief and fleeting. Our offerings will not allow our religion to be too ethereal and are constant reminders that God is the Lord of the earthy and mundane.

The offer of our lives is the best gift we can give. With the coming of Jesus, the priesthood with its elaborate system of sacrifices passed. Jesus was the perfect high priest who offered the perfect sacrifice. But sacrifices were not completely eliminated. Rather than making animal sacrifices, Christians were to offer their lives as living sacrifices.

Paul spoke of it this way: "I appeal to you therefore, brothers and sisters, by the mercies of God, to present your bodies as a living sacrifice, holy and acceptable to God" (Rom 12:1). No longer were animals slain and offered on altars, but human life was offered on altars of service. In a sense, worship reaches its climax when the worshiper says, "Here is my life, O God, weak, broken, and imperfect as it is. I lay it on your altar of service. Take it and use it as you can."

God's Word to the People

In Isaiah's experience of worship, God spoke. Isaiah knew he was addressed by God. It was as if he were being paged, as if God were calling him by name. Four words were spoken.

The first word was of judgment. Though not vocal, it was powerful in its silence and just as articulate as if it had been spoken. With this word of judgment, Isaiah was stricken with guilt. God is not morally neutral nor indifferent when it comes to evil and sin. God is not weak or sentimental. God is all-powerful, strong in holiness, righteousness, and justice; exposes the crooked ways of humankind; brings light to the darkness of human minds; and uncovers the corruption of our hearts. As God addressed Isaiah, God addresses us.

Overpowered by his guilt, Isaiah made two basic confessions of sin: personal and corporate. He could not stop with a personal confession but moved on to confess corporate guilt: "And I live among a people of unclean lips; yet my eyes have seen the King, the Lord of hosts!" (v. 5).

We are more conscious of personal guilt than we are of corporate guilt; personal confession is much more poignant and is sometimes made with tears and anguish. We are slower to make corporate confession, however, despite the fact that we are usually much more sinful in our corporate life than we are in our personal living. As a group, without shame and blushing, we do those things that would be repugnant and utterly distasteful in our more personal life. When do we hear of a family, an industry, a school, a community, or a nation confessing their sin? Seldom, if ever. Yet, in our public worship, ample opportunity should be given for the corporate confession of guilt as well as personal confession. So often our corporate sin is hidden in long-standing tradition and concealed in acceptable social behavior.

After his confession, Isaiah received forgiveness and cleansing. He seemed to have been standing near the altar, which may indicate that he was a priest. He told how one of the seraphim flew from the altar with a live coal in his hand and said, "Behold, this has touched your lip; your guilt is taken away and your sins forgiven" (v. 7).

Here we see the rhythm of judgment and grace, condemnation and forgiveness. This rhythm must be experienced in worship. Without grace, judgment is too harsh and devastating; without judgment, grace is cheap and sentimental. No word is more welcome than "Your guilt is taken away and your sin forgiven."

Following forgiveness and cleansing, Isaiah heard and responded to a call to service: "Whom shall I send, and who will go for us?" (v. 8). As God chose Isaiah, God still chooses followers for service on earth. We need to feel that we are the servants of God, that what we do on earth we do for the glory of God. This does not mean that we serve God exclusively by the altar or from the pulpit, but that we can press the simplest skills and most mundane tasks into God's service. We may faintly hear God's voice and dimly perceive God's purpose, but we can know great comfort in doing the divine will. When our work does not turn out right, and when the causes we have espoused fail, we are greatly strengthened in believing that God will not fail, and that God's will at last will be done on earth as it is in heaven. We may speak of serving community, nation, or global concerns, but all of these will sound hollow and empty unless we can feel that through them all we are serving God.

Finally, Isaiah heard the word of commissioning: "Go and say to this people." (v. 9) He was sent by God and under God's authority. Isaiah, like the other Old Testament prophets and the disciples and apostles of the New Testament, felt a strong sense of God's call. Pastors must also believe that God has called them to serve and given them a word to speak. This confidence can sustain them when all else fails.

The reading of scripture and preaching fall within the third movement of God speaking to the people. When we gather in our sanctuaries, believing that the God who has spoken in the past is not finished speaking, we hear again an eternal word that speaks to the contemporary situation. Although it comes out of an ancient past, it is fresh and contemporary, more relevant than the headlines of our daily newspaper, and proclaims a message much more important. It speaks to us in the valleys of life where we sometimes find ourselves: loneliness, separation, anxiety, sin, and death. The Bible holds out hope to men and women of all times and places. It speaks of grace, reconciliation, peace, forgiveness, salvation, and life.

Preaching is the sharing of those biblical truths that God has spoken through historical events, the prophets, and finally in Jesus. God still speaks the good news of the gospel through the lips of pastors, clothed in fresh language and addressed to the contemporary situation.

The People's Response

After Isaiah saw a vision of God, offered his own distraught life to God, and heard God speaking to him, he made a response to God's word: "Here am I! Send me" (v. 8).

We who worship God are not inert and lifeless, and we should not be passive. We are human beings who are capable of responding, and respond we should. Our minds should seek to grasp and understand the Word God speaks. Our hearts should exult in the good news, and we should pledge a faithfulness and devotion to God's message. We should desire to be doers of the Word, willing to be persons whom God sends into the world on missions of service.

Essential Experiences of Worship

If the four movements—seeing God, offering ourselves to God, hearing God's word, and responding to God's word—are incorporated into worship, essential experiences of worship will occur.

Experiencing God:
Transcendent and Immanent, High and Lifted up, yet Near

Like Isaiah, we must see God as high and lifted up, but close enough to touch our lips with grace. When God is visualized as completely transcendent, God is too far away and removed from the human situation. Yet, when God is thought of as altogether immanent, God may become lost in the shallow dimensions of our world.

While it is important to experience God as being near, we must experience God in a loftier manner—above the noise, confusion, and instability of our world. If God is truly transcendent, God will remain no matter what happens to our world. There is always the possibility of new creations, new beginnings, renewal, and rebirth.

The assurance of God's steadfastness is evident in a passage John Knox wrote in his autobiography:

> But if the worst should come and we destroy ourselves, whether in swift stages or in some total fiery debacle—even so, God's being does not depend upon man's fate on this planet. We know that, either late or soon, eventually this fate is death, as surely as death is the earthly fate of every man. But our faith and hope in God are not confined within this "bourne of time and place." Not merely from generation to generation, but from everlasting to everlasting, he is God; and in ways beyond our understanding and in worlds beyond our imagining he will fulfill the loving purpose of his creative work.[2]

I think that in the very earliest moment of worship pastors should help turn the hearts and minds of the people from themselves to a transcendent God who is holy, majestic, and loving. The call to worship, whether by the choir or pastor, can facilitate this effort. It should help the people lift their eyes and behold a God who is more than worthy of their worship and who invites their adoration and praise. An appropriate example would be: "Turn to me and be saved, all the ends of the earth! For I am God, and there is no other" (Isa 45:22).

The invocation is another crucial part of worship. While an invocation invokes the presence of God in the midst of the congregation, God should be addressed in such a way as to turn the minds of the people from themselves to God. A traditional invocation may be

> O eternal God, maker of Heaven and Earth, who stands above your creation like a craftsman above the thing he has made, we worship you. Wherever the farthest star which our most powerful telescopes cannot find, you are above that star. Stoop now in grace and be among us. Where we are weak strengthen us, where cowardly rebuke us, where sick heal us, where separated from our brothers and sisters reunite us, and where we are sinful forgive us. In the name of Jesus, our Lord. Amen.

Leading from the invocation is the first hymn. It should be carefully selected, helping the congregation to offer adoration and praise to God. It should be objective, a hymn that turns us from ourselves to God. Such hymns as "Holy, Holy, Holy," "Praise to the Lord, the Almighty," and "Praise the Lord, Ye Heavens Adore Him" meet this requirement.

Many worship leaders give attention to a balanced and integrated service where the hymns and anthems are centered around a theme usually determined by the sermon. This practice has value, but worship, like anything else, can be too balanced; after all, life is never perfectly symmetrical. In any case, the first hymn should not be used to integrate a service. Its relationship to the theme, if any, should be purely incidental. Its purpose is to turn the minds of the congregation to God.

Throughout the service, other hymns can be used, such as objective-subjective hymns that focus on God while appealing to the mind and heart. In evangelical worship where a strong emphasis is placed on decision, a subjective hymn, which appeals basically to the heart and will, can be used. All hymns, along with the call to worship, prayers, and other elements of worship, should help congregants better experience God as both transcendent and immanent.

Experiencing Judgment and Guilt, Grace and Forgiveness

In worship, we are brought beneath the judgment of God, which produces guilt in the most respectable of persons. I mentioned earlier how the "best" people, not the criminal and rabble-rousing elements, put Jesus to death. They were the kind of people we find in our churches on Sunday morning. How easy it is to infect our goodness with pride, to claim to be more and better than we are! The judgment of God pierces all persons with the pain of guilt, and few things are more destructive than unrelieved guilt. Yet, we do not despair in worship; grace is experienced, and forgiveness is offered.

I remember Curtis Brisson's saying, "When I went to the altar, my life was as heavy as a battleship; when I left, it I was as light as a feather." Rejoice in the words of Paul: "Where sin increased, grace abounded all the more" (Rom 5:20). There is enough grace in Jesus Christ to cover the sins of the entire world.

Experiencing Personal and Corporate Dimensions

Life moves between personal and corporate reality. We are persons, unique and different from anyone else on earth. In a world with its billions of people, our fingerprints are never duplicated. An individuality sets us apart from everyone else. Yet, our finest personhood and individuality are never achieved in isolation, but from the corporate life. We belong to each other. I cannot know who I am until I look into another person's face. We are bound together in a bundle of life. A solidarity holds us all together. In life's most solitary moment, there is a shuffling of feet. Somebody is going our way. We do not walk alone. Therefore, if worship is to be in touch with the great realities of life, the personal and the corporate dimensions must be experienced.

Isaiah's experience in the Temple was not in isolation. Others worshiped with him, and there—more than anywhere else—he remembered the history of the Jewish people and how God had dealt redemptively with them. Yet, the experience was very personal. His lips were touched by a live coal from the altar. It was as personal as if God had called him by name. He was in touch with the two great dimensions of life: the personal and the corporate.

We, too, worship with others. We are a part of the church that is a corporate reality. We speak of the church as a community of faith, a fellowship of the redeemed, and the body of Christ—these are all corporate descriptions. Yet, while we worship as a part of the corporate life, we should have moments of personal encounter with God, when God touches our lips with grace and calls us by name.

I remember talking with a young man at the close of a worship service. who said, "The service this morning was very personal. When you were about a third through your message, it was as if you and I were alone in the sanctuary, and you were talking to me." He experienced a personal meeting with God in the midst of corporate worshipers.

Experiencing a Return to the World

Returning to the world should not be casual, as if the experience of the sanctuary and that of the world were separate and disconnected. The experience of the worship is to be projected into the coming week. We turn to the world to be faithful to the vision we had in the sanctuary.

Isaiah could have lingered too long at the altar. The moment came, however, when he needed to leave it and go back into the world. He heard God saying: "Go and say to this people." Likewise, some of us hate to re-enter the world. We wish we could linger in the sanctuary with its vision, ecstasy, and joy. We recoil from the social demands of our religion. We had rather be on a spiritual high than in the lowlands of life. We had rather praise God than try to establish justice in the world.

We are often like Peter in the Transfiguration experience with its light, glory, mystery, and ecstasy. He did not want to leave the mountain top, so he said, "Lord, it is good for us to be here; if you wish, I will make three dwellings here, one for you, one for Moses, and one for Elijah" (Matt 17:4). Before he knew it, though, he was going down the rocky slopes of the mountain to its base, where he would find the sultry heat of the summer and human suffering with its pain and doubt. There he would find an epileptic boy undergoing a painful seizure of his illness and a father—caught between faith and doubt—who suffered more than his son.

Jesus said we are to be the salt of the earth and the light of the world. The purpose of salt is to save life from decay and give savor and taste to it. But if salt is to do its work, it must be in touch with life that is about to go bad. It cannot be aloof from it and cannot save itself in the process. It must lose itself. Light is to drive away the shadows and darkness of life, but to do this, it must make contact with the darkness.

I remember a neighborhood that was noted for its drunkenness, debauchery, and crime. Then a little church was established there. Its building was plain, and its members were simple ordinary people, but their lives were changed. They discovered the wonder of grace, the joy of being forgiven, a new sense of worth and dignity, and a deep awareness of the people who lived all about them. That church was not a barricade to the world. Rather, its doors opened to the world. Those who entered the doors for worship exited from them into the community to share their good news and offer themselves in humble service. There was a new moral tone, values changed, people had self respect, and relationships became more caring and nurturing. Someone said that the community changed so radically that one could see it in the way people kept their lawns. The church was salt, saving the community from decay; and it was light driving away the shadows and darkness. It portrayed the idea of the epistle of James that Christians should scatter into the world.

On a pew in the Congregational church in Brunswick, Maine, is a brass plate with this inscription:

> It was here while seated in this pew, listening to her husband preach, that Harriet Beecher Stow had the vision which led to the writing of *Uncle Tom's Cabin.*

In the light of worship she saw with greater clarity the terrible evils of slavery and was inspired to do something about it. Many such inscriptions could be put on the pews in churches across our land, honoring people who have seen their world in clearer light and gone out to help bring it a little closer to what God wants it to become.

Pastors have the privilege of leading people through worship to the presence of a holy and loving God who offers grace and forgiveness, communion with others, and opportunities for service in the world.

Notes

[1]Henry Sloane Coffin, *The Public Worship of God* (Philadelphia: Westminster, 1946) 16.

[2]John Knox, *Never Far from Home* (Waco: Word Books, 1975) 170.

Chapter 5

Make the Pulpit
a Place of Empowerment

Generally, when a pulpit search committee seeks a new pastor, it lists strong preaching skills as a prerequisite. Giving serious attention to the pulpit can preserve vitality in a church. It is tragic when pastors allow other tasks and responsibilities to crowd out thorough sermon preparation. They arrive at the hour of worship unable to speak a fresh, relevant, authentic word from God; the congregation remains spiritually hungry.

Churches who really love their pastor may tolerate poor preaching for a time. If they know the pastor is capable of better sermon delivery, however, but because of laziness and irresponsibility he or she fails to prepare, trouble results. What can make preaching consistently vital through the years? How can pastors be empowered to keep the pulpit a vibrant place in the life of the church ?

Preach the Bible

We believe that the Bible is the Word of God and that through it, God has spoken the most crucially important things about life. We also believe that God speaks in the hour of worship through the reading of scripture and proclamation of the Word. Preachers must be faithful to that Word, and their sermons must be biblically based. How do preachers select scripture and text that will prove faithful to what God has said? Passages should meet the following criteria.

Contains Mainstream Revelation/Great Biblical Themes

Christianity is a religion of revelation, the chief revelation being Jesus Christ. Therefore, Jesus Christ must be the touchstone in selecting scripture: Does it point to him, look back on him, reflect on him, or interpret him? Is the truth in keeping with who he was, what he did, and what he taught?

Preachers can easily misuse scripture, turn it into a kind of fetish or worship it, or be guilty of bibliolatry—which is another form of idolatry and very dangerous because it blinds people to the nature and purpose of the Bible. Jesus cautioned against worshiping the sacred scriptures:

> You search the scriptures because you think that in them you have eternal life; and it is they that testify on my behalf. Yet you refuse to come to me to have life. (John 5:39-40)

Proclaimers of the Word should consider if a selected scripture bears witness to Christ. If the passage is in the mainstream of revelation, then it will carry certain great themes of the Bible that re-occur like the theme of a symphony. They are not spoken once and then lost in silence.

Those who preach should look for five major themes:

(1) God—as creator and redeemer, just and loving, above us yet near; as the one from whom all things come, who is above all and in all, to whom all things move and find their end

(2) Jesus Christ—as revealer of God, Saviour, and Lord; his life, death, resurrection, ascension, present position at the right hand of the Father, and second coming to consummate history

(3) Holy Spirit—as God present in the world

(4) The Church—as the new Israel, community of faith, fellowship of the redeemed, fellowship of the reconciled, the people of God, the body of Christ

(5) People—their grandeur and misery, sin and fallenness, and possibilities when touched by the grace of Christ.

Other themes are forgiveness, reconciliation, liberation, salvation, the new life in Christ, faith, hope, love, service, the end of history, and the future life.

Speaks to the Human and Contemporary Situation

Preachers should consider the following questions that relate to the human situation when they select scripture: Does it speak to all people regardless of race, sex, class, nationality, and time in history? Does it seek persons in their anxiety, loneliness, separation, alienation, and sin? Does it overtake individuals as they walk in the shadow of guilt and into the night of death?

The Bible comes from a tradition and language that most people do not understand. It reflects customs and habits of life that seem strange and tells of people in history who have left behind their glory that now lies in the ruins of the past. Yet, the word of the Bible is transposable into the modern situation. It can be remarkably contemporary. Its voice can be very fresh and compelling. The Bible can speak at any moment in history, that place where no one has ever stood before and where no one will ever stand again.

In searching for scripture as the basis for sermons, pastors should ask such questions as:

•Is there some word for poverty, world hunger, and overpopulation?

•In a world of relativism where things are uprooted and adrift, where there are no points of reference except the shifting scenes of our time, does the text point to truths that can be lowered like huge anchors into the instability and turbulence of our culture?

•Is there a word of judgment against our materialism that even threatens to give a metallic ring to our souls?

•Is there something that can curb our greed that exploits nature, turning its resources into easy profits, that mars the beauty of our world, and that makes our earth sick with our refuse?

•Is there a word that can humanize the technology that threatens to destroy and devalue our lives?

•Is there some moral imperative that can lift the shadow of nuclear war that lies across the landscape of our world like an omen of planetary death?

•Is there a word of light for our darkness and some hope for our despair?

Speaks to the Pastor Personally

Preachers would do well to first ask themselves: Is the scripture a mirror in which I see my face? Is the gospel good news for me? Does the truth grip me? Does the text lift up hands begging to be preached?

When Paul Tillich was an old man, he delivered one of his most powerful sermons in Orchestra Hall in Chicago, with people crowded all around him. A young man rudely approached Tillich, brandished his Bible in Tillich's face, and belligerently asked: "Dr. Tillich, do you believe this book is the Word of God?" Tillich took the book from the boy's hand and said: "Yes! If the book grasps you, but not if you grasp it." I understand firsthand Tillich's implication, for I am not able to grip my people when I preach unless I have been grasped by the Word.

The pulpit becomes a place of empowerment when pastors select passages from the Bible that proclaim the revelation of Jesus Christ and speak to the human situation in its contemporary setting.

Experience the Gospel

While the mind is a wonderful faculty, it is not enough to only experience the gospel intellectually. Pastors, like the congregation, must personally experience the gospel and respond to it. They should hear the gospel speaking to the mind: "I want you to think me, grasp me, know how credible I am"; to the heart: "I want you to experience me, feel my wonder, and exult in me"; to the will: "I want you to live me, clothe me in flesh and blood, and incarnate me." Powerful preaching can result from that kind of response to the gospel.

Paul was a good student of the Holy Scriptures. He no doubt was familiar with Habakkuk and may have committed to memory one of the great verses of the book: "Look at the proud! Their spirit is not right in them, but the righteous live by their faith" (2:4). Though having an intellectual grasp of it, he never sensed the wonder until he experienced it.

He met the living Christ on the Damascus road and knew for the first time how spiritually bankrupt he was. He had nothing to give to Christ except empty hands. To his great surprise, Paul found out they were enough. Christ offered him salvation as a gift of grace. Paul only had to accept it by faith. He discovered a righteousness more wonderful than anything he had ever dreamed about—a righteousness of faith. His whole life changed when he experienced what Habakkuk meant, and out of that experience came Paul's two great doctrines: salvation by grace and justification by faith.

Martin Luther, who had an intellectual grasp of what Paul meant, underwent the same kind of experience 1,500 years later. Luther had been a scrupulous monk. He said of himself:

> I kept the rule of my order so strictly that if ever a monk got to heaven by his monkery, it was I. If I had kept on any longer I think I should have killed myself with vigils and prayers and readings and other work.[1]

He fasted until he was famished and would sleep without any cover at night until he shivered to the bone. Yet, he was always asking himself,

> Am I hungry enough? Am I cold enough? Am I deprived enough? Is there ever enough that will satisfy a holy and righteous God, and will constitute a claim upon God?[2]

Then he made the great discovery: *Sola Gratia!* Grace Alone! He discovered that he could not earn his salvation or stand before God as a just man in his own effort. By faith Luther responded to God's overtures of grace through Christ. His life was radically changed. From that experience, his slogan, "The Just Shall Live by Faith," shook Europe to its foundations, and the Protestant Reformation was born.

Almost 200 years later, John Wesley learned the same thing. In the Aldersgate experience his heart was strangely warmed, and he knew that God had forgiven even his own sins because of grace. Until then his preaching had been as dry as dust; after that it was like spring showers falling on dry and parched fields. That which he had known superficially became the great passion of his life.

Know the World and the People

A sermon that is biblically based has authority, but that authority is lost unless it is relevant and in touch with life. Pastors must know the world and people in it if their sermons are to make a significant impact. They would do well to sense the moods and temper, values and direction, questions asked and answers given, and the hope and despair of the community in which they live. They must live with the tension that has been created by two worlds, standing with one foot in the biblical world and the other foot in the modern world. Pastors must take the message that comes from a faraway past and transpose it into the twentieth and twenty-first centuries, taking images that seem strange to us and recast them into images the people understand. While the outward trappings of the two worlds are very different, their inward realities are very much alike. The basic problems of human life—anxiety, alienation, separation, sin, and death—endure the centuries.

Pastors who stand before a congregation on Sunday must have stood with those people during the week. They must know the community setting and family constellations to sense where the people are hurting and hoping, where their dreams have been dashed to pieces, and where hope is being reborn. The pastor must be able to speak to the guilt and shame of the parishioners, their sense of uselessness and worthlessness, their pride and prejudices, their fears and anxiety, their grief and sorrow, their conflict and estrangement, and their anger and hostility. Preachers must address the generous impulses of the people, as well as their kindness and desire to be better. Effective proclaimers will hold before the people what they can become when they are loved by others and touched by the grace of Christ.

Do Confessional Preaching

Confessional preaching is both testimonial and disclosive, positive and negative. In the positive sense, preachers can confess faith in Jesus Christ and bear testimony to what he has done for them. They will gladly tell people that the gospel is good news, not essentially in some intellectual and abstract sense, but in a deep, personal way. Like Paul they can say,

"By the grace of God I am what I am," (1 Cor 15:10) and "The life I now live in the flesh I live by faith in the Son of God, who loved me and gave himself for me" (1 Cor 15:10; Gal 2:20). Even when there is no verbal witness, there should be emotional overtones of joy, gladness, and gratitude that tell people of Christ's touch of grace that gives hope and life changes.

Confessional preaching can be negative by revealing personal weaknesses, prejudices and bigotry, and involvement in the sinful structures of the world. Yet, it becomes positive by breaking down barriers and building empathy between the proclaimers and the hearers, as evidenced in the following examples of Karl Barth and the apostle Paul.

Barth, the great Swiss theologian, preached for one year to prisoners in Basel, Switzerland. One day as he was preaching to the prisoners, he said:

> Let me tell you quite frankly, we are all together great sinners. Please understand me; I include myself. I stand ready to confess being the greatest sinner among you; yet, you may not excuse yourself from the group.[3]

Paul spoke of himself as no ordinary sinner but the chief of sinners. No matter what kind of audience he had, even if there were criminals in it, he could say, "There is no one here worse than I." Those who heard him would feel more grace than judgment and more identification than aloofness.

Make Effective Use of Illustrations

Preachers will never realize their highest potential without skillful use of illustrations. Persons in a congregation remember illustrations, though they may forget everything else in a sermon. Stories can paint pictures that thrust the truth into clear focus. Similes and metaphors can accomplish the same goal.

Jesus was one of the world's greatest storytellers. He knew the value of the story. He knew, for example, that it would be useless to talk about lostness in a tedious and prosaic way. If he had, those who heard it would have forgotten it almost as soon as they heard it. So Jesus told stories such as the one about the Prodigal Son.

Jesus was also skilled in the use of symbolic language. When he said, "You are the salt of the earth. . . . You are the light of the world" (Matt 5:13-14), he was using an illustration. He was creating visual images, making it possible for his hearers to see the truth. Those images became etched on their minds.

When Jesus said, "I am the gate. Whoever enters by me will be saved, and will come in and go out and find pasture" (John 10:9), he was using an illustration. He was talking about his uniqueness, though not using theological dogma. He was not talking abstractly, but was referring to something as concrete as a door. His hearers could almost see, touch, and handle the truth.

Allow the Holy Spirit's Guidance

The resources of those who preach are too meager, their moral vision is too blurred, their sensitivity is too dull, and their intellect is too limited to search out the deep things of God. They need help from beyond themselves. Such help comes in the person of the Holy Spirit. The Spirit can be illumination during sermon preparation as well as a powerful ally during sermon delivery.

Jesus referred to the Spirit as "the Spirit of truth" (John 14:17), the one who "will guide you into all the truth" (John 16:13), and "will remind you of all that I have said to you" (John 14:26). Pastors should never prepare a sermon or enter the pulpit without claiming the presence of the Holy Spirit. It will not come as a blinding light, but will gently illumine the truth and give empowerment for effective preaching.

Jesus experienced the Holy Spirit as power and promised that the Holy Spirit would be given as power: "And see, I am sending upon you what my Father promised; so stay here in the city until you are clothed with power from on high" (Luke 24:49)." But you will receive power when the Holy Spirit has come upon you" (Acts 1:8). This promise was fulfilled on the day of Pentecost when the Holy Spirit descended on the small group of Christians—all of them unpromising people—"like the rush of a mighty wind" from heaven.

The Holy Spirit is closely associated with preaching in the New Testament. Even Jesus felt the Spirit's power in his preaching. Luke tells us that after his temptations, "Jesus, filled with the power of the Spirit, returned to Galilee" (4:14). Peter probably preached the greatest sermon in the history of the Christian Church when 3,000 people were saved. Peter was not a preacher but a fisherman, an awkward and unlearned person. His sermon was given at Pentecost when the Holy Spirit came upon God's people. Paul certainly associated his power in preaching with the Holy Spirit. He had tried philosophy and eloquence of speech at Athens and had failed. Following that painful experience, he wrote to the Corinthian Christians:

> And I came to you in weakness and in fear and in much trembling. My speech and my proclamation were not in plausible words of wisdom, but with a demonstration of the Spirit and of power. (1 Cor 2:3-4)

The power of the Holy Spirit gives great hope to pulpits that are filled with squeaky lips and draggy feet and to sermons that lack life and vitality. How often preaching seems to fall upon stony soil! How frequently sermons are like spent arrows falling short of their target or like ricocheting bullets missing their mark! How badly preachers need the Holy Spirit's empowerment to go before them, turning minds into fertile fields for the planting of the word! Proclaimers of the Gospel should desperately long for the Holy Spirit to energize their words, guiding the truth they speak to the hearts and minds of the hearers.

Preaching biblical themes that speak to the human and contemporary situation, being grasped by the gospel in an experiential way, and standing with one foot in the biblical world and the other foot in the modern world will bring vitality to the church. In addition, confessional preaching, effective use of illustrations, and the guidance of the Holy Spirit will make the pulpit a place of empowerment.

Notes

[1]Timothy George, "Luther's Last Words: 'Wir Sind Pettler, Hoc Est Verum'" *Pulpit Digest* (September–October, 1983): 29-30.
[2]Ibid.
[3]Karl Barth, *Deliverance to the Captives* (New York: Harper Bro., 1959) 37.

Chapter 6

Learn Pulpit Language from the Bible

Pulpit language is often too spiritual, too pretty, too heavenly, and too out-of-touch with the common life. There should be something earthly about pulpit language. I expressed this opinion to a ministers conference some years ago. Some conferees were shocked. One man even thought I meant that preachers should be vulgar. Then I explained that I thought pulpit language should draw much of its imagery from the common experiences of life so that the congregation can understand and appreciate it.

While many good sermons have been forgotten because the language was bad, many bad sermons have been remembered because the language was good. What will help sermons to be remembered? Preachers can etch images on the minds of hearers and then infuse those images with feeling, many of which can come from the biblical literature types and language.

Use Simple Language

The Bible uses simple words to define God: "God is spirit," "God is light," and "God is love." Effective preachers follow the biblical example of using easy-to-understand language.

William Barclay has written of simple language: "I have always asked myself and other people: 'What do you mean by that?'" He told how John Wesley in his young days read his sermons to an old domestic servant, telling her to stop him every time he said something that she did not understand. As a result, his manuscript became masses of changes, alterations, deletions, and additions—but the sermons were intelligible. Barclay quoted Wesley:

> I design plain truth for plain people; therefore, of set purpose I abstain from all nice and philosophical speculations; from all perplexed and intimate reasonings; and, as far as possible, from even the show of learning. I labor to avoid all words which are not easy to understand, all which are not used in common life; and, in particular, those kinds of

technical terms that so frequently occur in Bodies of Divinity; those modes of speaking which men of reading are intimately acquainted with, but which to the common people are an unknown tongue.[1]

C. S. Lewis told about hearing a young preacher conclude his sermon like this: "And now, my friends, if you do not believe these truths, there may be for you grave eschatological consequence." After the service Lewis asked him, "Do you mean they would be in danger of hell?" "Why, yes," the young man replied. To this Lewis gave the cryptic response: "Then why didn't you say it?"

I was always pleased when the children and the simplest people of my congregation understood my sermons. We have made the mistake of believing that if something is profound, it cannot be simple. We should be wary of any truth that cannot be expressed simply; it may be spurious.

Use Concrete Language

Preachers would do well to tell about a loving person rather than read an essay on love, relate a certain kind deed rather than talk abstractly about kindness, or speak about a compassionate person rather than try to describe compassion. A church member would offer a great compliment if at the close of a service he or she said, "Pastor, you presented your truth in such a concrete manner that I felt I could reach out and touch it."

When Jesus talked about our tragedy of lostness, he did not use abstract language. He told about a lost sheep, a lost coin, and a lost son. There is nothing abstract about a sheep lost in the wilderness, or a coin misplaced in the dust and debris of a household, or a boy far from home and so hungry at sundown that he was tempted to eat the husk that the hogs left. In part, the concreteness of these stories has helped them to survive the centuries.

The Bible makes use of sensory language. For example, in his first letter, John appealed to the ear, eyes, and hands:

That which was from the beginning, which we heard, which we have seen with our eyes, which we have looked upon and touched with our hands, concerning the word of life. (1:1)

The Bible speaks about smelling the stench and putrefaction of life and tasting spiritual reality: "O taste and see that the Lord is good" (Ps 34:8).

Use Vivid Language

The Bible paints pictures with words to portray a truth and visualize certain ideas. Consider this parable:

> The Kingdom of heaven is like a mustard seed that someone took and sowed in his field; it is the smallest of all seeds, but when it has grown it is the greatest of shrubs and becomes a tree, so that the birds of the air come and make nests in its branches. (Matt 13:31-32)

Those who were with Jesus that day did more than hear the truth; they envisioned it.

An oral proverb says: "He is the best speaker who can turn ears into eyes." The late Peter Marshall advocated word painting in order that preachers might turn ears into eyes. I used a similar technique with my seminary students. I required them to write their sermons to achieve clarity of an idea. Then I encouraged them to review their sermons and make notations in the margins where ideas became visual. If no notations were in the margins, I insisted that they re-write the sermons until ideas became visual so their congregations would not only hear the truth but see it as well.

When I was a student in New York City in the early 1940s, I heard Joseph Sizoo preach. His church was about to be swallowed by a large secular city. Although only a few people were present for the service, Sizoo seemed to be inspired. It was as if he were painting a sunrise with words on an easel in the pulpit. When Sizoo came near the end of his sermon he said, "Once the dawn has started, nothing can stop it." I remember his sermon as clearly as if he had preached it only yesterday. Across the years in hours of discouragement, I have heard Sizoo saying, "Once the dawn has started nothing can stop it." If Sizoo had used more prosaic language, I would have forgotten the sermon before the night was over. Sizoo was an artist painting a picture with words.

Use Relational Language

The very essence of life is relationship. The tragedy of life can be expressed in terms of broken relationships and salvation in terms of broken relationships being healed. Christian theology is a relational theology that demands relational language.

Reconciliation is one of the great words in our theological vocabulary. It is about overcoming separation and estrangement and being reunited with the Creator. Such words as faith, trust, and love are relational. Faith is believing in somebody, trust is relying on someone, and love is giving of the self to another. Terms about the Church, such as the people of God or the body of Christ, are also relational.

Paul's words to the Ephesians remind us:

> Put away from you all bitterness and wrath and anger and wrangling and slander, together with all malice, and be kind to one another, tenderhearted, forgiving one another, as God in Christ has forgiven you. Therefore be imitators of God, as beloved children, and live in love, as Christ loved us and gave himself up for us, a fragrant offering and sacrifice to God. (4:31–5:2)

I have spoken of the need for fusion of mental images with feeling if sermons are to be remembered. If vivid language creates the image, then relational language provides the feeling. Such words as love, hope, forgiveness, trust, and life touch the springs of feeling in our lives. Vivid and relational language should be combined in preaching.

Use Mostly Nouns and Verbs

Psalm 23 has only four adjectives and two adverbs. The story of the Prodigal Son uses only nine adjectives and eight adverbs. It is interesting that no adjective is used to describe the father in that story. I would have heaped adjective upon adjective in describing him: loving, accepting, affirming, gracious. Only one adjective—angry—is used to describe the elder son. I would have been tempted to lavish adjectives on him:

arrogant, proud, selfish, harsh, judgmental. I would have told how legalism had dried up the springs of compassion in his heart.

If preachers use the example of the Bible, they will choose nouns that are strong and sturdy and verbs that are vigorous and colorful. Nouns and verbs will carry the weight of truth in sermons with little need for adjectives and adverbs. Effective sermons will result and bear fruit.

The Bible provides many examples of simple, concrete, vivid, relational, and action language. Such biblical language tells how good news is best communicated by its proclaimer.

Note

[1]William Barclay, *A Spiritual Autobiography* (Grand Rapids MI: Eerdmans, 1975) 26.

Chapter 7

Use Imagination in Preaching

J. H. Jowett stressed the importance of the imagination in preaching:

> I am urging the cultivation of the historical imagination, because I am persuaded that the want of it so often gives unreality to our preaching. If we do not realize the past we cannot get its vital message for the present. The past which is unfolded in the pages of Scripture is to many of us very wooden: and the men and the women are wooden: we do not feel their breathing: we do not hear them cry: we do not hear them laugh: we do not mix with their humanness and find that they are just like folk in the next street and so the message is not alive. It does not pulse with actuality. It is too often a dead word belonging to a dead world, and it has no gripping relevancy to the throbbing lives of our own day, and so I urge you to cultivate the latent power or realization, the power to fill with breath the motionless forms of the past.[1]

The Imagination

Imagination is the power to form mental images of objects not present to the senses. Use of imagination requires dealing with reality that lies beyond the five senses of hearing, seeing, touching, tasting, and smelling. The imagination is boundless and almost limitless. It is not hedged like the mind, heart, and will.

The mind comes upon frontiers of mystery it cannot cross over. The heart can tolerate just so much pain and ecstasy. The will is always running into walls it cannot climb. The imagination is not limited by time and space. It can roam the universe, yet, drift into destructive fantasy if it is not tethered to reality. The healthy imagination stays in touch with reality, despite occasional daydreaming.

The Bible's Use of Imagination

The Bible has many fine examples of how the imagination can be used creatively. In Isaiah 6 the author talks about the transcendence of God but never says God is transcendent. That would have been an abstraction without color, concreteness, and vividness. Instead, he talks about a transcendent God in images and pictures:

> In the year that King Uzziah died, I saw the Lord sitting upon a throne, high and lofty; and the hem of his robe filled the temple. Seraphs were in attendance above him; each had six wings: with two they covered their faces, and with two they covered their feet, and with two they flew. And one called to another and said: "Holy, holy, holy is the Lord of hosts; the whole earth is full of his glory." (vv. 1-3)

Psalm 104 is about God and nature. God is nature's creator, and nature is God's servant. The Psalmist made creative use of imagination by talking about God and nature in images and pictures:

> You art clothed with honor and majesty, wrapped in light as with a garment. You stretch out the heavens like a tent, you set the beams of your chambers on the waters, you make the clouds your chariot, you ride on the wings of the wind, you make the winds your messengers, fire and flame your ministers (vv. 1-4)

The best use of the imagination is in the Book of Revelation.

> The wall is built of jasper, while the city is pure gold, clear as glass. The foundations of the wall of the city are adorned with every jewel;. . . and the twelve gates are twelve pearls, each of the gates is a single pearl, and the street of the city is pure gold, transparent as glass. . . . The nations will walk by its light, and the kings of the earth will bring their glory into it. Its gates will never be shut by day—and there will be no night there. (21:18-19, 21, 24-25)

These wonderful images represent reality. But what kind of reality? Heaven will be beautiful with the richest and fullest kind of life. The imagination often grasps truth and reality beyond the reach of the mind.

Imagination and Preaching

Preachers should properly use the imagination in the pulpit. The imagination is indispensable for effective preaching. It appeals to the dimensions of wonder, mystery, the unseen, and the eternal. It allows preachers to transpose themselves into historic situations and describes what it sees in images and pictures, not in abstracts.

There are lateral, forward, upward, and backward movements of the imagination in preaching. Lateral movement enables travel to any place or event. Time and distance are transcended. Forward movement involves futurism—telling what will be happening in ten or twenty-five years. People need both warning and hope for the future, and preachers can help give them both. Upward movement of the imagination is the type John had on the Isle of Patmos when he saw the new heaven with the new Jerusalem: "And I saw the holy city, new Jerusalem, coming down out of heaven from God, prepared as a bride adorned for her husband" (Rev 21:2). Sometimes the human heart can be so badly broken only a transcendent vision can bring healing. When family members see a loved one lowered into the grave, they want to believe that one day they will be united with their loved one and family ties will never be broken.

Backward movement of the imagination is most helpful for preaching. With its use ministers can re-create the historic situation as accurately as possible through the use of commentaries and other helps. The worship leader can help the congregation to identify with the people in the story—to see with their eyes, hear with their ears, feel with their hearts, and touch with their hands; to experience their prejudice and bias, pain and brokenness, hopes and fears, and deep insatiable longings of their hearts. Skillful use of this movement will almost set proclaimers of the Word as eye-witnesses.

Examples of how to effectively use the imagination in preaching may be the doctrines of redemption and justification. Paul took the term redemption from slavery. One day he was passing a slave market. There was nothing strange about this since slave markets were found everywhere. The young man being sold caught Paul's attention. He was rosy-cheeked and fine-looking. He was no ordinary person. The marks of aristocracy were on him. He was the kind of person who could be a writer, a teacher, an artist, or a statesman. He was obviously well-born and well-bred. He and his family had likely been the victims of war, carried away, and sold as slaves. Paul thought to himself: "What a waste of life!"

The bidding began. On the edge of the crowd was a soft-spoken man who was topping the bids. No matter how high the bid, this man always bid higher. When the bidding was over, he took his purchased slave and began moving away from the crowd. Paul's curiosity was very great, so he began following them. He heard this humanitarian say to his slave: "I have bought you to freedom. I have redeemed you. Go now, you are a free man." Paul thought: "This is exactly what Christ has done for us, yet in a much more wonderful way. He has set us free from the terribly enslaving powers of sin and death."

I told this imaginary story about Paul one Sunday morning when I was a guest minister at one of the churches in our community. At the close of the service a man, who was reputed to know more about the Bible than anyone else in the congregation, asked me "Where did you find that story in the Bible?" I had to confess that it was not there but that it was about one of the great themes of the Bible. It could have been in the New Testament.

Paul took the terminology of justification by faith from the courts. I remember one of my most enjoyable pastimes as a boy was to go to the courthouse when court was in session. I enjoyed hearing the lawyers argue their cases. Then in suspense I listened for the verdict of the jury and the sentence passed by the judge.

I have a feeling that Paul was like me as a boy. The Roman court was off-limits to him since he was a Jewish boy, but he probably slipped in and listened to the lawyers argue their cases. He must have remembered one particularly dramatic trial when he waited with bated breath for the judge's decision. The suspense was finally broken when the judge said: "I declare this man just before this court." Paul could not forget that statement.

One day when he was mulling over the court decision, it occurred to him that God had done exactly that for him, yet in a much more wonderful way. When he believed in Christ, God said, "I declare you a just person before me since you have believed in my Son." He then understood the concept of grace and justification and proceeded to teach it to others by using common terminology. He demonstrated how that using the imagination responsibly, keeping it tethered to reality, can lead to lively and powerful preaching.

Note

[1]J. H. Jowett, *The Preacher: His Life and Work* (Grand Rapids MI: Baker Book House, 1977) 124-25.

Chapter 8

Be an Evangelist, a Nurturer, and a Prophet

Pastors are called to three basic roles: evangelist, nurturer, and prophet. To neglect any one of the three is to have a crippled ministry.

Evangelist

The term evangelism means "good news." Therefore, the evangelist is the one who announces the good news. The good news begins with the claim that the world belongs to God, who loves it and cannot give it up. No matter how broken, sinful, and rebellious humans are, God's love remains. God has come to us in Jesus Christ, the revealer of God and the messenger of love, forgiveness, and salvation.

Evangelism is like telling the sick they can be well again, showing the hungry where there is food, and pointing the way home for the lost. D. T. Miles described evangelism as one beggar telling another beggar where to find bread.

The evangelist is like a guard at the end of a long, bitter night announcing: "The night is almost over. I see faint streaks of light in the east. Day will soon be here. The darkness will soon be driven away, the mist will be lifted from the hills, and the shadows will be scattered in the valley." The evangelist knows the day is a day of good tidings. The evangelist will share both the good and the bad news.

In the Beecher Lectures on preaching at Yale Divinity School in 1977, Frederick Buechner discussed the role of evangelist in literary terminology: *Telling the Truth: The Gospel as Tragedy, Comedy, and Fairy Tale.* The evangelist must bear the bad news that we are sinners. Having lost our way, we stumble through darkness to our death. This is the gospel as tragedy. Yet, we are loved, cherished, and sought. That is the good news and the gospel as comedy. The gospel becomes a fairy tale with the good and extraordinary things that come to sinners because of God's love.

The pastor as evangelist takes his or her role-model from the New Testament. It contains parts of four sermons: Acts records two by Peter, one by Stephen, and one by Paul. The sermons by Peter and Paul are quite evangelistic, and Stephen's sermon has strong evangelistic overtones. It should be no surprise that New Testament preaching was basically evangelistic. Did not Jesus once describe his mission in evangelistic terms? "The Son of Man came to seek out and to save the lost" (Luke 19:10). Evangelism in the New Testament was more than preaching, however.

Today we need a more adequate concept of evangelism as well as a more adequate language with which to define it. Growing up in eastern North Carolina, we were thinking evangelistically if we spoke of souls being saved. Years later I realized that Jesus did not talk this way; neither did Paul nor the New Testament. Jesus and the New Testament envision the redemption of the total life. Zacchaeus is a good example.

Zacchaeus, after entertaining Jesus for dinner, said: "Look, half of my possessions, Lord, I will give to the poor; and if I have defrauded anyone of anything, I pay back four times as much" (Luke 19:8). Can you imagine Zacchaeus going to town the next day? He probably met a lot of people he had cheated across the years. To one man he said: "Four years ago I cheated you of five pounds. Here are twenty. I am restoring four to one." To another he said, "I swindled ten pounds from you only last year. Here are forty." He told another person, "Many years ago I took fifty pounds from you unlawfully. I have felt so guilty. It has been a heavy burden to bear. Here are two hundred pounds. Take them!" It is doubtful that anyone said: "Did you hear about old Zacchaeus? His soul was saved." More likely, the townspeople commented in awe about the great change in Zacchaeus—how he treated others and how giving he had become. He had experienced the ministry of the great evangelist, Jesus Christ.

Nurturer

Perhaps the ultimate end of the pastor's work is to nurture believers into Christian maturity. Without this nurturing, persons remain like infants. As a result, marriages fail, human relations are tortured, and churches live under tension.

Jesus looked at his generation and concluded that the problem was immaturity.

> But to what will I compare this generation? It is like children sitting in the marketplaces and calling to one another, "We played the flute for you, and you did not dance; we wailed, and you did not mourn." (Matt 11:16-17)

He remembered the children playing in the streets of Nazareth. The games started with such zest and enthusiasm, but the playing broke into petty wrangling and quarreling. His generation was like those children.

Later in the New Testament days, the church at Corinth experienced the problems of Christian immaturity. The church had parties and factions that fought and wrangled, though the divisions were merely symptoms of the underlying problem of immaturity. Paul wrote: "I fed you with milk, not solid food, for you were not ready for solid food. Even now you are still not ready" (1 Cor 3:2).

Paul had a great deal to say about growing up. "But speaking the truth in love," he wrote, "we must grow up in every way into him who is the head, into Christ" (Eph 4:15). We could wish that Paul had elaborated on this concept, but obviously maturity had something to do with loving as Jesus did—affirming, accepting, and caring for others, and being as concerned about the welfare of others as oneself.

It is no accident that one of Paul's most striking statements about maturity is a part of his great chapter on love (see 1 Cor 13:11). We can substitute the concept of maturity for love in that chapter and not do violence to the truth: "The mature person is patient and kind; the mature person is not jealous and boastful. The mature person is not arrogant or rude, does not insist on his or her way, and is not irritable or resentful."

Love leads to the heart of ethical power. Love is the cardinal Christian virtue. The pastor as nurturer must lead persons to develop such virtues.

Prophet

The prophet is not one who uncovers hidden and esoteric knowledge. While there may be a futuristic element in prophecy, the primary function of a prophet is not to predict the future, but to address the contemporary generation. The pastor as prophet speaks both a word of judgment and a word of hope. Since God is a God of justice, one must speak a word of judgment. But because in God there are also the springs of mercy and re-newal, the prophet should speak a word of hope.

The eighth-century Hebrew prophets knew the importance of speaking both a word of judgment and hope. For example, Amos' withering word did not spare the marketplace with its dishonesty, marriage with its infidelity, the courts with their miscarriage of justice, the temple with its deadening formality, or society with its corruption. Yet, in the end Amos still held out hope for his nation: "I will plant them upon their land, and they shall never again be plucked up out of the land that I have given them, says the Lord your God" (9:15).

Prophetic preaching can be a corrective to other kinds of preaching, particularly evangelistic preaching, which has often had a dark and sha-dowed side and has been too comfortable in the presence of social evils that degrade and destroy human life. Evangelists have cried out against personal sins and neglected the social ones. Preaching has been little more than pious platitudes. We have needed the prophetic cutting edge.

The prophet has always been at risk and has never been safe in any place or generation. Remember the words of Jesus: "Jerusalem, Jerusa-lem, the city that kills the prophets and stones those who are sent to it" (Matt 23:37). So we have to ask: How can a pastor preach prophetically and survive?

In the 1960s I attempted to address the problem of racism, especially as it existed in the church. I told the congregation we could not be the church of Jesus Christ and close our doors to people whom Jesus loved, for whom he died, and whom he had accepted. If we did, we would sim-ply be a social club, not a church. I survived those difficult years and learned that two things were necessary for survival: a deep trusting rela-tionship with my people and confessional preaching.

I had good relationships with my people. During my twenty years of service with them, I had walked with them through the shadows of lone-liness, sickness, and death. I had been with them in the mornings of success and joy. I loved them, and they loved me.

I believe this mutual love and respect will allow the prophetic voice of a pastor, although agreement between all parties may not always re-sult. As time goes on, however, some persons may wonder if the pastor is correct in his or her thinking. At that time, the pastor can begin to change attitudes and values of the members of the congregation.

During the turbulent 1960s, I acknowledged that I was caught in the sinful structures of our world just as my people were. Psychologically, often I left the pulpit and went to the pew to make my confession with the congregation. I would begin a sermon with "I confess that I have been a great racist. I know how wrong I was. I have asked God's forgiveness, and God has given me peace." My preaching contained judgment, but it was the judgment of a fellow-confessor, which is the most effective kind.

The pastor as nurturer will aid in the development of closeness with the congregation. Deep relationships, in turn, can absorb the shock of the prophetic voice, and confessional preaching will save the evangelistic preacher from the image of a severe judge. The world needs authentic pastors who will give balanced attention to the role of evangelist, nurturer, and prophet.

Chapter 9

Search for the Authentic Church

In the New Testament, over 100 images point to the authentic Church. We must confess that often the church is not authentic, however. It stumbles through the world, not sure of its direction, and imbibes too deeply at the fountain of its culture. It uses spiritual language and performs religious functions, but it is essentially secular at heart.

Let us consider four of these images: the church as the people of God, the church as the reconciled fellowship, the church as servant, and the church as the body of Christ.

The People of God

The continuity between the Old and New Testaments is best seen in the overriding concept of the people of God the, clearest indication of which is found in Exodus 19:5-6:

> Now therefore, if you obey my voice and keep my covenant, you shall be my own treasure of all the peoples. Indeed the whole earth is mine, but you shall be for me a priestly kingdom and a holy nation.

The people of Israel were puzzled as to why God chose them. They were the smallest of all people and not especially gifted; they were stubborn and rebellious. Israel was chosen because of God's grace (see Deut 7:7-8). As the people of God, Israel found her identity. When the little country was overrun and the people were scattered in a strange land, Israel never completely forgot she was special to God. This great truth made sense of her history and gave her hope for the future.

The same idea of the people of God persists in the New Testament. Note the similarity of both idea and language in Peter's statement to that found in Exodus:

> But you are a chosen race, a royal priesthood, a holy nation, God's own people, that you may proclaim the mighty acts of him who called you

out of darkness into his marvelous light. Once you were not a people, but now you are God's people; once you had not received mercy, but now you have received mercy. (1 Pet 2:9-10)

Peter spoke of the Church's beginning—from being nobodies to becoming God's people. The journey was long, but it was made in grace.

One of the most difficult and important tasks I had as a pastor was to understand the principle of being God's people and to teach it to the congregation. If we are the people of God, we should display the spirit, integrity, and character of Christ, our liberator. Paul in his letter to the Philippians wrote: "Let the same mind mind be in you that was in Christ Jesus" (2:5). What does it mean to have the spirit and integrity of Christ? "By this everyone will know that you are my disciples, if you have love for one another" (John 13:35). The embodiment of agape love comes nearest to telling us what we should be. We are to love people and the world the way Jesus did.

A Fellowship of Reconciliation

The great tragedy of humankind is estrangement—from God, others, ourselves, and progressively from nature. The Bible offers the remedy to estrangement: reconciliation with God and others. The classical statement on reconciliation is found in 2 Corinthians 5. Here the primary mission of Jesus is defined in terms of reconciliation: "All this is from God, who reconciled us to himself through Jesus Christ" (v. 18). Note that it was the world, not God who was being reconciled.

Paul's world was similar to ours: It was hostile and divided. Threatening and yawning chasms lay across that world such as socio-religious (Jew and Gentile), socio-economic (master and slave), and socio-sexual divisions (men and women—with women as decidedly inferior). Paul said that Christ had spanned those chasms and reconciled the hostile and divided people: "There is no longer Jew nor Greek, there is no longer slave nor free, there is no longer male nor female; for all of you are one in Christ Jesus" (Gal 3:28).

From Paul's point of view the most threatening of the three chasms was the socio-religious division between Jew and Gentile. They despised each other. Paul proclaimed the good news that Christ had come to reconcile them, and the sphere of reconciliation would be his body, the church. In Ephesians Paul said that Jews and Gentiles had been reconciled through the cross. They had stacked their arms of warfare at the foot of the cross and become one—a new people in place of the two factions of warring and hostile people. Christ had created "in himself one new humanity in place of the two, thus making peace" (2:15). They had been reconciled "both groups to God in one body through the cross, thus putting to death that hostility through it" (2:16). The irreconcilable was reconciled in the church.

Reconciliation is the primary mission of the church. Unfortunately, many pastors are tempted to become peacekeepers rather than peacemakers. They spend a majority of their time quenching fires of conflict in the church, mollifying hurt feelings, and keeping a shallow peace in the fellowship rather than seeking true reconciliation. Remember: Jesus did not say "Blessed are the peacekeepers," but "Blessed are the peacemakers."

Servant

The disciples would never forget the night Jesus asked for a basin of water, tied a towel around his waist, and went to all of the disciples, washing their feet. He dramatized the fact that he was a servant and that those who follow him are to be servants also. Because Jesus saw himself as a servant, he never misused his power or authority. Freely he gave it up and finally suffered the ultimate humiliation of the ancient world, death on a Roman cross. He was a suffering servant who gave his life for the life of the world. The authentic church follows the model of Christ. It is not above its Lord. It must not be too proud to wash and dry the dirty feet of the world nor too squeamish to swab its running sores.

The Body of Christ

Paul's favorite metaphor for the church was the body of Christ as portrayed in 1 Corinthians 12. He designated three characteristics of this body: (1) It is many but one. (2) Each member, even the weakest, is indispensable. (3) It is a shared life. The church is more than brick and mortar, more than organizations and budgets, and more than numbers and statistics. The church is a living body, just as Christ, its founder, was a living being.

Christ wants to continue his ministry through the church. The church is to be his hands and feet, eyes and ears, and mouth and voice. He wants to comfort the sorrowing, feed the hungry, and heal the sick through the church. Paul wrote: "There are many members, yet one body" (v. 20). The authentic church allows and encourages individuality and diversity. It seeks the finest gifts in a person's life and then tries to develop them to their fullest potential.

While the body has many limbs and parts, it is one. If, like in the human body, the parts do not work in unity, the body is not well. Paul said that even the smallest and most insignificant part is indispensable: "On the contrary, the parts of the body that seem to be weaker are indispensable" (v. 22). This is true of the authentic church. It takes the poorest, most unsophisticated, and most unlikely member and says, "You are indispensable. We couldn't be who we are without you." What could give a person greater dignity?

I remember a week of preaching in a church not too far from where I live. The church had a substantial membership with some of the finest and most important people of the community on its roles. The one person I remember was a mentally handicapped man in his early forties who stood at one of the doors of the sanctuary, warmly greeting people and handing out church bulletins. That church could not be what it is without him. If he should move away from the community, something of the church would move with him, and when this poor man dies, something of the church will die as well. Each member is indispensable!

Finally, the life of the Church as the body of Christ is a shared life. Paul said: "If one member suffers, all suffer together with it; if one member is honored, all rejoice together with it" (v. 26).

I once attended a conference at the Seventh Day Adventist Medical Center in Washington, D.C. I shall never forget what one of the doctors said: "If a nerve is injured, the whole body rushes to that nerve to heal it." The same is true of the authentic church. If one of its members is sick whether physically, emotionally, or spiritually, the church will surround the person with love and caring in an effort to bring healing. If a person is grieving, the church says, "We will not let you weep alone; we will weep with you." If a member is suffering, there are words of comfort: "We will not let you suffer alone; we will suffer with you." In times of joy the church offers affirmation: "We will not let you celebrate alone; we will celebrate with you." The body of Christ is a shared life.

During the hostage crisis of 1985 in Beirut, Lebanon, an American plane was hijacked. Several members of a Catholic congregation in Algonquin, Illinois, were aboard that ill-fated plane, including two of their priests who had led a group to the Holy Land. Because of the dramatic nature of the circumstances, television allowed us to observe the worship of that church. We saw a distressed and grieving congregation saying silently to their unfortunate members "We will not let you suffer alone; we are suffering with you." One of the priests returned earlier than expected. In his first sermon to the congregation he said, "When the hand hurts, the whole body suffers. When one suffers in the church, we all hurt—because we are Christ's body."

The authentic church—the people of God, the body of Christ—offers reconciliation, servanthood, and support for all its members and reaches out to those outside the congregation. Pastors who seek an authentic church will teach and lead toward understanding of these concepts.

Chapter 10

Hold on to Humanness

We often say in jest: "There are three kinds of people: men, women, and preachers." There is, however, a note of seriousness in this joking. Many people do, in fact, see ministers as being different—not really human. But ministers *are* human. To deny their humanness is to do them a disservice as well as the people they serve. Humanness can be a great asset to pastors.

The Pastor as Human

Ernest Mosly wrote:

> Regardless of our degree of spiritual commitment, we need to remember that we are all subject to all the intellectual, moral, ethical blunders of human persons. If we forget that, we may became competitors with God instead of children who worship and follow him.[1]

Pastors are human. They are dependent on a goodness, grace, and love they cannot claim in and of themselves. Dependence leads to God, one of the religious sources of life. Pastors, like others, must live by grace and gifts not of their own creation.

Pastors are also interdependent. They need family and friends. They are incurably social and need hands that reach out and touch them, voices that call them by name, and feet that strike cadence with them and walk with them. Because of their humanness, pastors need people who love and affirm them, who accept them as they are, and see possibilities in them they cannot see in themselves. When they have lost faith in themselves, they need people who believe in them and who will trust them.

In acknowledging their humanness, ministers must accept that they are fragile, weak, often tempted, sinful, and will inevitably die. They must allow themselves to accept strange contradictions in life: laughing and weeping, love and hate, hope and despair, belief and doubt.

Accepting humanness means accepting physical realities: a body that needs food and rest and drives of hunger, thirst, and sex. Holding on to humanness means recognizing the presence of strong feelings and expressing them honestly.

Finally, embracing humanness means acknowledging deep longings for goodness and beauty. In their best moments, ministers know that to be truly human is to be loving, caring, and compassionate.

Temptations of Humanness

Pastors may be tempted in two directions: to live above humanity and to live beneath its best possibilities. They may assume a kind of suspended position somewhere between heaven and earth and may appear not to be tempted the way other people are. They may wear a kind of halo and be unduly shocked by and judgmental of the frailty and common failure of others. As proof that they are different, ministers may develop a spiritual pomposity with a holy voice and pious manners.

Pastors may be attracted to the suspended position because of its safety. In it, they are out of touch with people and not so vulnerable. To be vulnerable is to take down defenses, remove guards, and be genuinely open to people. It means openness to acceptance and rejection, affirmation and denial, pain and joy, and wounding and healing. Vulnerability means taking risks.

While the suspended position may keep some ministers safe from vulnerability, it also imposes a sense of loneliness. It removes them from the common traffic, the jostling of ordinary life. It takes them away from people and precludes the possibility of deep relationships. Ministers who choose the suspended position find the ministry to be a lonely profession.

The suspended position is not only safe and lonely; it is false. Pastors are human, and anyone and anything that denies this reality is deceptive. Projecting a false self can cause ministers to break under the tension between who they really are and who they appear to be. They may become depressed, suffer a nervous breakdown, or in a terminal illness be unable to conceal their fear of death. In such a crisis, the false image is exposed.

People can become disillusioned when, having had such an exalted and unrealistic image of ministers, they see how human they are. Emerson told about hearing a preacher who was so false and unreal, that he was sorely tempted to neverattend church again.

A snowstorm was falling around us. The snowstorm was real; the preacher merely spectral, and the eye felt the sad contrast in looking at him, and then out of the window behind him into the beautiful meteor of the snow. He had lived in vain. He had no word intimating that he had laughed or wept, was married or in love, had been commended, or cheated, or chagrined. If he ever lived and acted, we were none the wiser. The capital secret of his profession, namely, to convert life into truth, he had never learned.[2]

Historians report that Captain James Cook, the British explorer, lost his life because he allowed the people of Hawaii to think he was a god. While Cook was in harbor for the first time, the natives thought he was a deity, and Cook did nothing to discourage them. After accepting their deification, he left the harbor and sailed into a fierce storm where his ship was blown and battered. When he returned to the harbor, the natives were puzzled. How could such a fate have overtaken a god? Feeling betrayed, they attacked the ship and killed the captain.

Something of a much milder nature may happen to pastors who fall from their exalted position, causing people to see their humanness. I knew a pastor, revered by his congregation and respected by the community, who became terminally ill with cancer. He could not conceal his fear of impending death. The reaction of persons in his church was very telling and interesting: Some seemed shocked, some were angry, some were disappointed, and still others were disillusioned. Of course, all were hurt. Had he not preached on the resurrection, eternal life, and life beyond the grave? Had he not told them that Jesus Christ had conquered death and that everlasting life is a present reality. Why was he so afraid? The reaction of his people might have been different if he had told them that he knew he would be afraid when the time came for him to die. If he had made a simple confession that he believed he would recoil from the loneliness and anguish of death like Jesus did, people would not have been so shocked. A simple declaration of his humanness could have made a difference.

While I have labored the point of the pastor's attempt to be more than human, the other temptation is to be too human. This can be just as dangerous as the other one. Some ministers may jump from their false pedestal and be too eager to show how dirty their feet are. They may go out of their way to prove how human they really are. They may resort to cursing, telling risque jokes, or drinking alcoholic beverages, and wash their "dirty linens" in public. The temptation to strip themselves too bare in the pulpit will inevitably injure them and embarrass the congregation. After all, we do not have to work too hard at proving our humanity.

Humanness as an Asset

One of the greatest assets of pastors is the acknowledgement of their humanness. It puts them in touch with reality. Denial of temptation, anger, jealousy, depression, and other human traits are sure signs of unhealthy mental and spiritual posture. Expressing humanness can open ministers to experience the grace of God. They must realize their own efforts are not good enough. Like their parishioners, pastors must acknowledge their unworthiness in accepting God's gift of grace.

Admitting humanness opens ministers not only to God, but to people. It strips away the masks of disguise and tears down the facade of hiding. To confess personal hurt, loneliness, fear, and sorrow is to strike responsive chords in the hearts of others who experience the same thing. Rather than being driven apart, pastors and congregations are drawn closer. Self-disclosure can result in an atmosphere of warmth and acceptance.

Expressing humanness can make preaching more effective. Next to the grace of God, it can be the greatest asset in the pulpit. Only persons who know the grace of Christ can tell others of that grace. Only saved sinners can tell other sinners where grace and forgiveness can be found. Only those who have been wounded and had their wounds healed can tell others where they can be cured. Only pastors who know they must die can exult in the hope of the resurrection and preach the Easter message with power.

Admitting human qualities can help ministers accept ministry from others. Most pastors are slow to acknowledge their physical, mental, emotional, spiritual, material, and other needs. Every pastor needs a pastor, but only as pastors accept their humanity will they allow others to be their pastor.

I remember a serious crisis early in my ministry that was provoked by gossip about me. Fortunately it was false, the creation of a sick mind. I needed help. Who could help me? Who would be my pastor? Finally I turned to my family doctor who had no shallow marks of piety on him. He was rough and tough on the outside, but warm and human on the inside. I still remember the day he came by the parsonage with his Bible. He read from 2 Peter and told me how he had been the victim of gossip. Then he affirmed me in a very warm and caring way. He was a good pastor to me and never knew how healing he was.

Effective pastors cannot deny their humanness. They cannot live above it or beneath it. Admitting human weakness can be a great asset in opening the doors to ministry by and to pastors.

Notes

[1]Ernest E. Mosley, *Priorities in Ministry* (Nashville: Convention Press, 1978) 12.

[2]J. H. Jowett, *The Preacher: His Life and Work* (Grand Rapids MI: Baker Book House, 1977) 103.

Chapter 11

Keep a Vigil
over all Areas of Life

Some people believe pastors are above temptation. They may, in fact, be tempted more than anyone else. Pastors are tempted by spiritual pride. The ecclesiastical way is littered with pastors who have made wreckage of their lives. They may have been idealistic dreamers and extremely gifted at one time but were overcome by temptation.

Paul confessed: "But I punish my body and enslave it, so that after proclaiming to others I myself should not be disqualified" (1 Car 9:27). He was afraid that some unchristian behavior would discredit him, and that the message of grace and acceptance would be rejected. Most pastors share Paul's fear of their ministry being discredited. Lest they mar their high calling and bring shame upon it, they must keep a vigil over the physical, intellectual, moral, and spiritual areas of life.

The Physical Life

Our biblical faith does not see a dualism between the soul and the body. The body is a whole; the body is one. It locates sin not in the body but in the will. Some religions have seen the body as sinful. God looked upon creation and said that it was good. Our bodies with their drives of hunger, thirst, and sex are good. We can make evil from these natural desires, but they are not evil within themselves.

A Greek heresy taught that salvation was in terms of the soul being delivered from the body. We do not see salvation only in terms of the soul being saved. Instead, the Bible teaches redemption of the whole life, even the body. Salvation will not be complete until the perishable nature puts on the imperishable nature, and the mortal nature puts on immortality (see Rom 8:23; 1 Car 15:53).

No religion has had such a high concept of the body as Christianity. Paul wrote: "Do you not know that your body is a temple of the Holy Spirit within you, which you have from God? (1 Cor 6:19). The body is a temple in which the Holy Spirit dwells. Such a temple should not be violated.

We are called to be good stewards of our bodies. Yet, doctors tell us that ministers are notorious abusers of their bodies. Like everyone else, they should eat the right foods, take proper exercise, get sufficient rest, and avoid compulsive work habits. Since Sunday is the busiest and hardest day for pastors, they should take a day of rest during the week for physical, psychological, and spiritual renewal. As part of their overall attention to health, pastors should spend adequate time with their family members and involve themselves with family activities. Living close to nature also contributes to physical well-being.

The Intellectual Life

If pastors are to love God with their minds and avoid intellectual sloth, a program of continuing education is essential. It is indeed sad to see pastors who deteriorate intellectually in the pulpit. This is a common death for many pastors. They lose their intellectual curiosity, fail to read stimulating books, do not observe a rigorous study schedule, and cease all serious efforts at further education. Graduation from college or seminary should not be seen as the completion of education, but rather as a prelude to continued learning. Formal education should be seen as providing skills and tools that will enable ministers to be productive students in the future.

Minds that are not stimulated can grow stale and lose freshness and vibrancy of ideas. A stale mind produces stale language and ideas that have lost their vibrancy. Pastors who do not continue to study will produce sermons that are poorly thought-out and shabbily constructed. Ideas will be artificially put together, not relating in any organic and living way. The sermon will be wooden and lifeless. Or, these pastors will go frequently to the sermon barrel and lift sermons they have preached before, with no attention to re-working the sermons or making them contemporary. Some persons may even preach the sermons of other preachers without giving proper credit.

I once attended a conference for ministers that featured outstanding biblical scholars, theologians, preachers, and church administrators. I was excited about the prospect of hearing a particular well-known preacher. When he began to preach, I felt as if I had heard the sermon before. After the worship service, a friend of mine confronted the speaker and accused him of preaching one of his sermons. I knew why the sermon sounded so familiar: I had read my friend's sermon. The preacher that night not only used my friend's ideas, but he told the personal experiences as if they were his own! When word of the confrontation reached other conferees, a pall fell over the meeting. I felt this was true partly because the speaker's plagiarism had caused guilt in many of us who had also used the sermons of other preachers.

A program of continuing education can contribute to a long pastorate. During my ministry with First Baptist Church, I went away each year for study. The congregation appreciated the fact that I would take the time and make the effort to better prepare myself for ministry. They felt it was one way in which I was affirming them, and I thought they were more than worthy of the best that I could give them.

One of the old influential churches of our city was looking for a pastor. The chairman of the pulpit search committee asked me if I had a word for him. I told him to let the prospective pastor know of the committee's expectation for church-funded, yearly study of the pastor's choosing. I emphasized the importance of continued intellectual growth.

The Moral Life

Congregations want to believe in and love the pastor. It is unfortunate when pastors, because of immorality, betray the trust of the people. Church members will show signs of hurt, bitterness, and disillusionment as a result. Christian morality includes honesty, truthfulness, acting responsibly, and loving and caring for people the way Jesus did. The example of that morality should be both lived and preached by pastors.

I was a student in New York City in 1941. Jack Dempsey, the former heavy-weight boxing champion, had a restaurant on Broadway. When I was on Broadway, I always walked by that restaurant, hoping to see Dempsey. Often I saw him having coffee with friends. One day as I was approaching the restaurant, I saw a mass of people looking in. I was curious, so I elbowed my way through the crowd to get a better view. I saw Dempsey with two midgets. What a contrast!

In 1943 I was in the army in North Africa. At the first worship service I conducted—held in a cork forest near Rabat—I preached on Christian maturity and told the story about Jack Dempsey and the midgets. At the close of the service a sergeant, who had served many years in the Army, came up to me and said, "Chaplain, don't you know that story about Jack Dempsey and those midgets is a lie?" The officer had no reason to doubt me since he had never seen me before, but he obviously had a distrust of the pulpit. He had heard preachers whose integrity he questioned. Probably a shadow lies across the pulpit for more people than we would like to acknowledge. They have heard preachers who were not faithful to the truth.

When I was a first-year theological student, I heard a preacher of international reputation tell of his visit to the Cathedral Church in Copenhagen, Denmark. As he and his guide were walking down the aisle toward the altar, they were so overpowered by the magnificence of the sanctuary that they dared not speak above a whisper. As they moved toward the altar, the guide whispered, "At the altar is Thorwalden's famous statue of Christ. If you would see the face of Christ, you must kneel at his feet." The preacher said, "At last I stood before that statue of Christ whose head was bowed. Then I dropped to my knees and looked up into the loveliest face I had ever seen."

A few years ago I was in Copenhagen and visited the famous Cathedral Church. I had expected to stand before the statue of Christ with bowed head, and then drop to my knees and look up into the loveliest face I had ever seen. When I arrived at the altar, I saw the statue standing on a three-foot pedestal. I did not have to drop to my knees; I had only to look up into the lovely face. I realized that the famous preacher had been caught up in the desire to be dramatic in the pulpit and had overshot the truth. Truthfulness is an important part of a minister's ethics.

I think often of the moral life of Jesus. His temptations were not coarse and vulgar. He was simply tempted to use power that a servant cannot use, and he was a servant. Ministers are plagued by the same moral temptation. They are constantly in danger of abusing their power by using and manipulating people.

One of the crudest forms of human exploitation is sexual manipulation; and unfortunately, sexual promiscuity is widespread among ministers. The church will forgive other sins, but never sexual infidelity of pastors. Ministers who are guilty of this sin are quickly forced to leave their church. Vigil over the moral area of life was neglected, and many people suffer as a result.

The Spiritual Life

Harry Emerson Fosdick once wrote: "Prayer is the soul of religion itself in its inward and dynamic aspect of fellowship with the eternal."[1] Some persons may feel that Fosdick overstated his case, but there is great truth in his words.

Jesus, our model spent much time in prayer. He prayed privately and publicly, spontaneously and liturgically, and faced every crisis in prayer. We too should go from the presence of God into the presence of others; this double action is impossible without prayer. A daily devotional life will help prepare pastors for leading public worship on Sunday as well as for ministry throughout the week.

Following are suggestions for ministers to recapture the sense of wonder and mystery in all areas of life.

(1) Study the devotional literature of the Bible, especially the Psalms.

(2) Become acquainted with some of the classical books on the devotional life such as Augustine's *Confessions*, Richard Baxter's *The Reformed Pastor*, Wesley's *Journal*, Brother Lawrence's *The Practice of the Presence of God*, Thomas á Kempis' *The Imitation of Christ*, and John Baille's *A Diary of Private Prayer*.

(3) Saturate the mind with devotional hymns such as: "Jesus, Thou Joy of Loving Hearts" and "O Master, Let Me Walk with Thee."

(4) Practice prayer as communion with God and not as a way of getting things. I stated earlier the need to spend time in God's presence before entering the presence of others.

Keeping personal vigil over the physical, intellectual, moral, and spiritual life will enable stability and effectiveness in pastorates. A well-balanced lifestyle is essential for pastors as they seek to confront daily human temptation and weaknesses.

Note

[1]Harry Emerson Fosdick, *The Meaning of Prayer* (New York: Association Press, 1946) xi.

Chapter 12

Take the Drudgery out of Administration

Many pastors chafe under the responsibility of administration. I have often heard them say: "I like preaching, counseling, and in general the pastoral task, but I hate administration. It is the bane of my existence." Administration is like a shadow over ministry that threatens to take the joy away. While administration is drudgery, it nonetheless persists. How can pastors see administration in a new light, think of it as indispensable, and make it creative and challenging and something they enjoy? How can they take the drudgery out of administration?

Administration as Indispensable

Administration is essential to the life of a church, although it is often viewed negatively. Many people want religion, like a spring, to be bubbly, free, and uninhibited—but without cutting a channel. They do not like structure and the administration that goes with it; they want only spontaneity under the Spirit's leading.

I think the religious movements in our time that have taken place outside the institutional church have something to say to us. In part, the leaders have rebelled against the church with its forms, structures, and administrative tasks. They have viewed the church as a warrior dressed in armor that is too heavy, or a dried-up river bed, or a mausoleum that has form and beauty but not life. Yet, these groups cannot completely escape the administrative task. Sooner or later they need a treasurer. Somebody has to collect the funds and pay the bills, or a committee has to be appointed to find a new place for their meetings. The bubbly spring has begun to cut its channel.

Administration has been with the church from its very beginning. Jesus sent the disciples on a mission. Organization was involved; they were sent two by two (see Mark 6:7; Luke 10:1). Paul was a great preacher and missionary statesman, but also was an effective administrator. He always left behind a church with people who had clearly defined responsibilities. His administrative ability helped channel and preserve the tremendous results of his preaching. On his first missionary journey, he appointed elders in the churches he had founded: "And after they had appointed elders for them in each church, with prayer and fasting they entrusted them to the Lord in whom they had come to believe" (Acts 14:23). In mentioning the eight gifts of the Spirit in 1 Corinthians 12, Paul designated the seventh gift as "administrators."

John Wesley followed the biblical example of gifted administration. He left behind closely knit societies that became the basis of the present-day Methodist Church. Like other spiritual leaders, he demonstrated how indispensable administration is to the life of the church.

An Adequate Concept of Administration

Often we set administration in strictly organizational dimensions that are too narrow and restrictive: preparing budgets, organizing fund-raising, authorizing purchases, paying bills, keeping records, promoting attendance, and maintaining grounds and buildings.

Schaller and Tidwell gave this concept of administration:

> Administration is enabling the children of God who comprise the body of Christ, the church, to become what, by God's grace, they can become, and do by God's grace, what they can do.[1]

In helping the children of God to become what they should be and the church to become the instrument God can use in the world, pastors are called to lead churches to use available resources to accomplish the mission of the authentic church.

The church's resources are physical, human, and spiritual. Physical resources are buildings, grounds, furnishings, and equipment. While the physical resources are accessories to the church and do not determine its basic nature, they are important. They are to the church what tools are to the carpenter. Tools cannot build a structure, but in the hands of a carpenter they are indispensable.

Human resources are people with their talents, gifts, and financial strength. The church is people gathered around Jesus Christ in worship, faith, love, and service. If the members are inept, spiritually insensitive, and do not understand the nature and mission of the church, they will be like an unmotivated and unskilled carpenter who does not know how to use tools. The quality of the people will determine how the physical resources will be used.

Spiritual resources are the Bible, the Christian faith, the gospel, and the presence of the Holy Spirit. They make the church unique and different from all other institutions. Use of all three types of resources helps to achieve the authentic end of the church.

The Pastor's Unique Role as Administrator

Pastors should know how to organize a church, draw up a budget, and promote a church program. They have a unique role in the administration of the church. Pastors who want to fulfill this unique role and discover the excitement of administration should do administration pastorally and theologically.

The pastor/administrator cares for people and helps them grow and mature as part of the administrative task. From the pastor's point of view, administration should not allow organizations and structures to become ends, but the means of developing people.

Ernest E. Mosley told about a great day in his life:

> A significant change occurred in my ministry in 1962, I became aware I was performing my pastoral duties in Pali View Baptist Church, Kaneoke, Hawaii, like a "doer of things"; rather than a "grower of persons."[2]

Most pastors are tempted to be doers of things rather than growers of persons. They would do well to evaluate themselves by these standards: Do I use people to achieve organizational goals, budgets, promotional ends, and statistics? If I do, then I am a doer of things. Do I use buildings, organizations, budgets, promotion, and statistics to build up people? If so, then I am a grower of people. Simple administrative assignments can help persons discover and develop their gifts.

In addition to doing administration pastorally, pastors should learn to do it from a theological interpretation of the church's nature and mission. The pastor/theologian will help persons understand what it means to be equipped to be God's people in the world, and then will help channel their energy and vitality toward achieving this theological ideal.

I am reminded of the day when the architect who designed our new church building told me he wanted the architecture and symbolism to express basic tenets of the Christian faith. He asked for my ideas or theological interpretation. I remembered how Paul spoke of the death and resurrection of Jesus as being the heart of the Christian gospel (1 Cor 15:3-4). The gospel was like an ellipse with the death and resurrection of Jesus as the two foci. I asked the architect if he could represent that symbol in the architecture. He said he would suspend a cross from the ceiling of the chancel and transcend the cross with a resurrection window. These symbols are powerful in announcing the gospel of the church.

As my church's lead administrator, I also had the opportunity to give a theological interpretation of the church in the late 1960s during a racial crisis in our community. An association for mentally handicapped children was looking for facilities for a school. Request after request had been refused because there were some black children in the group. I began thinking about our new, modern educational building that lay idle for most of the week, so I called the chairman of the association to offer some of our facilities if the church would approve. I received mixed reactions when I presented the idea to our deacons. One man was vehemently against his grandson attending a racially mixed school. At our next meeting, however, he was the first person to confess that he had been wrong. The church eventually approved the idea.

During that racial crisis, I tried to explain what it was to be the people of God in our community at that particular time. I said we were to be the love, compassion, and acceptance of Christ in Martinsville, that Jesus would have taken those children into his arms and blessed them, and that we could not refuse them and be the people of God. The day our church opened its doors to those children was the day it was most like Christ.

Pastors can take the drudgery out of administration by viewing it as an indispensable task that can help the church to be God's people through the use of all available resources. Pastors have the unique opportunity to lead through care-giving and theological interpretation of the mission of the church.

Notes

[1]Lyle E. Schaller and Charles A. Tidwell, *Creative Church Administration* (Nashville: Abingdon Press, 1975).

[2]Ernest E. Mosley, *Called to Joy* (Nashville: Convention Press, 1973) 7.

Chapter 13

Learn Creative Conflict Management

One of the most difficult problems pastors face is conflict management. Most pastors have asked themselves: How can I prevent conflict? How can I bring about reconciliation? How can I prevent people from being hurt? When people are hurt, how can I help heal them? How can I make conflict creative? How can I become skilled as a manager of conflict? Many pastorates are short-lived because the pastor is awkward in handling conflict, while longer pastorates reflect pastoral skill in conflict management.

The Reality of Conflict

Conflict within the church is an inevitable reality. It may be among the members, between the pastor and the church, or both. Conflict is certain because many people are unduly sensitive and easily hurt. Some are frequently threatened and become defensive, while others are overly ambitious and seek power and positions of leadership. Personality clashes are almost endless; some people simply do not like each other and are disagreeable.

Churches can develop profiles of conflict and may have a history of it. Remarks such as these are not uncommon: "They can't get along in that church; they are always fighting." "The Smiths have always run that church." "That church has always run off its pastor."

Pastors who develop profiles of conflict have short pastorates. They can never really enjoy a honeymoon period with the church and early become embroiled in conflict. The church is seen in an adversarial role from the very beginning. The cause of conflict can be either church members or pastors or both.

Conflict does not have to be destructive. It may be like a surgeon saying: "When this leg heals, it will be stronger than ever." When they are properly handled, relationships can become stronger than ever. Pastors can be instrumental in conflict management.

The Pastor and Conflict

Most pastors handle conflict in one of three ways: They attack, run away, or stay and deal with it responsibly. Pastors who attack are often aggressive, belligerent, confrontive, accusative, and intimidating in dealing with conflict. The style of leadership displayed by such persons cannot be effective. It widens the chasm between individuals, causes deeper opposition, and creates new wounds and aggravates old ones. Pastors who attack during conflict wound the church, injure their families and themselves, and may even destroy their ministry.

Pastors who choose to run from conflict refuse to acknowledge and confront it. When conflict is too obvious to be ignored, they may observe its raging from a safe position or give the false hope that the problem will be solved. Running from conflict displays a lack of strength or courage to lay a firm hand on the situation, give direction to it, and bring about peace and reconciliation.

Pastors who face conflict responsibly do not attack or run away. They are not surprised by conflict and understand it as a part of humanness. They believe conflict can be resolved creatively and in ways that will not be too harmful.

Managing Conflict Creatively

Following are seven suggestions for pastors who seek to manage conflict creatively rather than attack their opposition or run from a confrontive situation.

Be a good listener.

Listen with concern and be non-judgmental. Be willing to hear petty, trivial complaints; understand that they are important to those who make them. Such listening is therapeutic and drains anger and hostility so that emotional wounds can heal. Lead the church to become a listening church.

Keep the channels of communication open.

Encourage conversation about the issues to clarify them and prevent attack and counter-attack. Once anger is siphoned off in non-destructive ways, the issues do not seem to be so serious. Wonderful things can happen when people honestly face their differences openly and talk about them in reconciling ways.

Stand firm on significant moral and spiritual issues.

Most church fights begin with small matters, such as the kind of rug for the parlor, the placement of a piano, or the color scheme for the sanctuary. Such disagreements touch off latent hostility and re-open old wounds and make new ones. People continue to fight long after the original issue has been forgotten. Wise pastors will not involve themselves with these matters, but will stand firm on great moral issues.

I know a pastor who lost his church over the racial issue. Someone asked, "On which side did he stand?" The reply was, "Neither. He chose to be neutral and got squeezed in the middle." During a storm, the safest place to stand is on the side of some great moral principle, even though it may seem the most vulnerable and dangerous position at the time.

Accept hostility as inevitable and do not return it.

Sooner or later most pastors will be the objects of hostility and will be tempted to strike back when attacked. To manage conflict constructively, mature and secure pastors will refrain from returning hostility.

Richard Baxter offered some wise counsel for ministers in dealing with enemies:

> Contend with charity, but not with violence; set meekness, and love, and patience against force . . . . Speak not stoutly or disrespectfully to anyone; but be courteous to the meanest, as to your equal in Christ.[1]

Dietrich Bonhoeffer once said:

> The man who despises others can never hope to do anything with them.
> The faults we despise in others are always, to some extent at least, our
> own too.[2]

Booker T. Washington gave sound reasoning for not returning hostility. He said that he would allow no person to drag him so low as to make him hate that person.

Allow church members to be right.

Acknowledge that their ideas may be the best ones. Do not take personal affront. Parishioners will admire and respect pastors who are open to new ideas, trusting, and mature.

Do not take sides with a group in the church.

Even though one group may share the pastor's viewpoint, the pastor should not side with that group in opposition to others. This does not mean that all groups are equally right, and pastors are to be morally neutral. Pastors can state their moral and ethical convictions in ways that do not put them in alignment with one group and in opposition to another. Pastors are thus agents of reconciliation.

Be loving, caring, accepting, affirming, and reconciling.

Pastors who see themselves in the role of reconciler and peacemaker will heal many wounds and prevent many quarrels. Philips Brooks said wisely in his Lyman Beecher Lectures many years ago:

> There are such things as parish quarrels. If I am right my friends, you
> will never have one which you might not have prevented, and never
> come out of one without injury to your character and your master's
> cause.[3]

While I am not sure pastors can prevent every parish quarrel, I believe Brooks was essentially correct in his judgment.

Peacemaking pastors can make conflict creative that will result in stronger relationships. Through reconciliation ministers can help members understand each other on a deeper level and experience the meaning of grace, forgiveness, acceptance, and affirmation in a fresh and new way.

Hindrances to Effective Conflict Management

Personal qualities can prevent pastors from being effective healers of conflict. Insecurity, immaturity, manipulation, and irresponsibility in conversation are among these.

Insecurity

Insecure pastors will be unable to handle conflict; they will constantly feel threatened. Insecurity may cause them to attack or retreat. Pastors who are very insecure may become paranoid, feeling that members—particularly those who are in positions of power—are against them. These pastors are the kind who feel they must be present for all deacons' meetings and committee meetings. They are suspicious and distrustful, so they want to be present to defend themselves or to see that nothing is done without their knowledge. In extreme cases, if they are pushed hard on a particular issue, they may say to the church: "If you don't pass this, then you can have my resignation." Conflict remains.

Immaturity

Immature pastors cannot handle conflict constructively. In fact, they will probably cause conflict rather than heal it. Such persons may be hotheaded and impulsive. They get mad easily and may pout, sulk, or ignore people. They may say to a committee: "If that's the way you feel, then handle it yourselves."

One of the main objectives of pastors should be to lead the people to emotional and spiritual maturity. Paul spoke about attaining

> the unity of the faith and of the knowledge of the Son of God, to maturity, to the measure of the full stature of Christ. We must no longer be children. (Eph 4:13-14)

But how can pastors lead the congregation in this direction if they themselves are immature? Immaturity thereby blocks the road to building better relationships.

Manipulation

Manipulation is using people as means to ends or as tools. This practice is very dehumanizing, and sooner or later they react against it. Some pastors, rather than serving the church, may want the church to serve them. They may use the people as stepping stones in the march to success.

Pastors have the kind of authority as God's messengers that makes them vulnerable to manipulation. They may be tempted to present a new program to the people saying, "I am sure this is of the Lord. This is God's will for you." Actually, the program may not be of God at all, but born of overwhelming pastoral ambition. The stage is set for conflict.

Irresponsibility in Conversation

Many pastors talk too freely. It is tragic to see pastors become bearers of tales or even gossipers. Pastors should be careful about talking among church members. They should never speak about anyone unless their words are affirming, nor should they divulge confidences.

I remember a woman of our community calling me one day and saying, "I have a problem that I would like to discuss with you. I am not a member of your church, but if I discussed it with my pastor, all of Martinsville would know about it by sundown." Such pastors stir up trouble rather than heal conflict.

Practical Suggestions

Pastors have no control over some interrelationships and issues. They must accept binding ties within the church, among family members and friends, and in the community. Pastors can control some involvement with potential conflict, however, by limiting the power of their position and removing themselves from initiation of some ideas.

Realize that some hostility originates outside of the church.

The winds of hostility are often blown through the windows of the church from other sources such as the home, business, industry, social relations, and personal frustration. Many people often find it impossible to deal with anger at its source, but they are able to vent it in the church. In an odd sort of way, this can be a great compliment to the church.

Understand the deep ties that often lie hidden in a church.

Such ties may be in the family, or social, economic, or political in nature. They are especially present in old, established churches and will remain through various pastorates. These ties are often involved in conflicts pastors may experience with the church. Some persons may rally around the pastor in initial skirmishes. Yet, as tension mounts, these same people grow more and more aloof. If there is a final showdown, they may not support the pastor at all and perhaps will even vote against him or her. The pastor is confused, hurt, and angry.

Pastors who find themselves in this scenario must understand that their friends had to decide whether or not to support the pastor, thereby running the risk of having the ties strained and broken. Usually church members choose to keep the ties, where they find much of their identity and security. Ties are deeply imbedded in the life of a church, and pastors should be aware of them lest they run blindly into them and get hurt.

Do not preside over church business meetings.
Do not present controversial recommendations.

Pastors should never preside as moderator. Also, if they feel strongly about an issue, they should enlist a strong and trusted leader in the church to present controversial recommendations. Thus, the threat of pastoral power is removed.

Refuse the power of hiring and firing staff members.

I heard a pastor say recently that a church is always hurt when a staff member is fired. No matter how unsatisfactory the staff member may be, he or she always has friends and a following. When pastors assume the power to hire or fire, sooner or later they may discover that their relationship with the church is no longer tenable.

Pastors must accept the inevitability and dynamics of conflict within the church. Those who, through personal growth, learn to manage conflict creatively will enjoy deeper relationships and longer pastoral tenure.

Notes

[1]Richard Baxter, *The Reformed Pastor* (London: The Religious Tract Society) 37-38.

[2]Dietrich Bonhoeffer, *Letters and Papers from Prison* (New York: Macmillan, 1958) 25.

[3]Philips Brooks, *Eight Lectures on Preaching* (London: SPCK, 1959) 103.

Conclusion

The preceding chapters are written with the conviction that most pastorates are too short. Often pastors do not stay long enough to build deep and trusting relationships, without which pastorates cannot be creative and fulfilling. While the book is not an autobiography, it does have an autobiographical flavor. From reflections on a forty-year pastorate, I would like to reemphasize certain ingredients that I consider essential for long pastorates that have life and vitality.

(1) Even in the face of failure, pastors must be assured of God's call to preach. God has given them a word to speak that is so important that neither the proclaimer or hearer can live without it.

(2) The most holy task of pastors is worship leadership. They are called to lead people into the presence of a holy and loving God to whom praise is offered.

(3) Pastors must fulfill three basic roles: evangelist, nurturer, and prophet. The evangelist follows the example of New Testament proclamation. The nurturer guides persons to mature life in Christ, a life that reflects the love of Jesus. Like the Hebrew prophets and Jesus himself, the prophet addresses the corporate life: speaking of judgment, justice, and hope.

(4) Preaching should receive special attention. The pulpit can be a place of empowerment from which God's message is inspired by the Holy Spirit. The use of appropriate pulpit language and a creative imagination can make the truth come alive.

(5) Pastors should search for the authentic church. The danger in the modern church is that while performing a religious function, it remains essentially secular at heart. Ministers must return to the sources of New Testament faith and make them contemporary.

(6) Holding on to human qualities is one of the greatest assets of ministers. Pastors should strip away halos and relax false postures, but without making wreckage of their lives. While maintaining their humanness, they should keep a vigil over all areas of life.

(7) The ministry requires practical skills in administration and conflict management. Pastors must acknowledge that administration is indispensable and can be used to help develop the gifts of persons. Similarly, conflict is inevitable; thus, pastors should seek to manage it so as to minimize hurt and develop stronger relationships.